African Americans and Other Myths

Confusing racism with cultural diversity.

by Kenneth Brooks

Amper Publishing, Vallejo, California.

African-Americans and Other Myths

Confusing racism with Cultural Diversity

Copyright © 1994 Amper Publishing Co.
First Printing 1994
Second Printing 1998

All rights reserved. No part of this book may be reproduced in any form or by any electronic or mechanical means, including storage and retrieval systems, without permission in writing from the publisher, except by a reviewer who may quote brief passages in a review.

Library of Congress Catalog Card Number: 93-73899
ISBN 0-9639042-3-X

Amper Publishing Co.
Post Office Box 882
Vallejo, CA 94590-0088
(707) 554 3515
book@amperpublishing.com

This book is dedicated to my parents Oscar and Anna May Brooks. They taught me that determination, sound moral values and self discipline are the basis for the good life.

Preface

Writing this book forced me to question my assumptions about group labels. I had to reconstruct my thinking along the way. I had to leave behind familiar and comfortable racial images. They distorted my self-image. Even so, it was hard to erase them from my thinking because of habit.

This book shows how many oppressed people actively help in their own oppression. They are addicted to patterns of thinking that confuse their normal human instinct for self preservation. They are unaware of or resist the intellectual, emotional and behavioral changes needed to free them from self-defeating thoughts. A distorted history creates an environment conducive to confused thinking.

The thinking errors referred to in this book are applicable to people in many oppressed groups. It could have been written from the point of view of women, Native Americans, or any ethnic group that faces oppression in America. I chose to use the experiences of brown-skinned people of African descent for three reasons. First, because their oppression is the most documented and the most flagrant. Secondly, because other groups have copied their methods and attitudes of fighting oppression. Third, because many of my insights come from my own experiences as a brown-skinned person in a color conscious society.

Throughout the book, I use the terms black, white, African-American and European-American to show current thinking. A statement like "the `black' community," is a means of showing current attitudes and not my own. Color based discrimination is a book topic, so I had to refer to people's skin color. For purposes of physical identification I use the terms brown-skinned, dark-skinned and pale-skinned. They imply no stereotypical images.

Throughout the book, my intention was to provide information that will help people see history and culture differently. I hope it will motivate readers to question how America uses group labels to control people. I hope it will generate discussion about the nature and use of culture.

Thanks to Kwenu Brooks for his suggestions for

improving my book. His role as devil's advocate was helpful in revealing the weak points in my thinking and keeping me intellectually humble. Thanks to Diana Cubit who offered suggestions for improving the book. She suffered through hours of dialog as I struggled toward my new beliefs. I thank Dawn Dolan for testing the arguments in the book against critical thinking standards and for her suggestions in improving the writing.

Table of Contents

Introduction 3
   The Plan 3
   Goals 6
      Setting Goals 7

Battle For Control of the Mind 9
   History of Enslavement 9
   European Slaves 17
   Europeans as Morally Superior 22
   Thinking 30

African-Americans 31
   Cultural Influence 41
   Label 43
   Culture and History 48
   Black-Americans 52

IMAGE 63
   Rights As Citizens 66
   Power To Make Change 67
   Americans of African ancestry. 72
     Destructive Thoughts 73
   Attitudes 77
        Black Culture 77
        Black Correctness 84
        News Reporting 94
        Hair 100
        Internal Group Relationships 101
        Standards 102
   Education and History 105
   Change 110
   Separatist 113

Discrimination and the Law 117
    Ineffective Laws 117
    Discrimination as a Criminal Offense 122
    Law Enforcement Control 130
    Police Support 133

Conclusion 137

African Nations List 142

European Nations List 143

Constitutional Amendments 144
    Amendment XIV 144
    Amendment XV 145
    Amendment XIX 146
    Amendment XXIV 146

Selected Bibliography 147

Endnotes 149

Be Free

What can be sadder
Than to be imprisoned in one's mind

To have the gift of awareness
Wasted, caged in a dull mind
Covered in a blanket of ignorance

Open your mind to knowledge
See the world differently
You only need to think
Think to free yourself

Humans are forever imprisoned
When they fail to use the gift of awareness
When they refuse to open their minds
Accept new thoughts
And

Be Free

Introduction

Introduction

The Plan

American citizens of African ancestry can live a positive life in the United States of America. They can free themselves from most of the emotional burdens that come with being people of color living in a predominant pale-skinned race conscious society. They can realistically expect things to improve in the future. In spite of all the negativity and despair revealed after the 1992 Los Angeles uprising, there is a chance for a positive future. We can only bring improvement by changing from the old ways of defeatist thinking.

We need a plan for ending systematic oppression in America. We need it now. Unless one is devised soon, the plight of Americans of color will get worse.

Americans with darker shades of skin coloring face daily physical, legal and economic exploitation. Some examples of abuse are:
1. police abuses
2. harsh criminal sentences
3. civil rights abuses
4. poor legal services
5. inadequate health care
6. substandard schools
7. inadequate city services
8. employment discrimination
9. home loan discrimination
10. business loan discrimination
11. historical role distortion

What we don't realize is the even more damaging constant assault on our spiritual and emotional health. Since the government instigates or at least condones much of this abuse, we cannot rely solely on it for salvation.

The enslavement, murder, discrimination and genocide practiced against Africans, their descendants, and other people of color are recorded in America's history. Thousands of books document these abuses. This book shows ways to help reverse this tide of oppression. It helps oppressed citizens discover patterns of distorted thinking. New approaches for fighting oppression and regaining our rights and privileges are revealed.

Oppressors discriminate against us because of our skin color or sex. They have restricted freedoms, caused emotional suffering, and trapped many in cycles of economic stagnation. "Be patient," says the power group." Work hard, pay your dues, prove yourselves and eventually you'll achieve your full citizenship rights." Then they laugh as we beg and plead with them to give us what already is ours.

They enjoy using their privileges and ours too. Why should they hurry change? If we're too lazy, ignorant or uninspired to take back our citizenship rights, we should not be surprised when they keep them. Thieves and outlaws usually do not voluntarily return stolen goods.

Historians, sociologist and politicians write about the plight of the "Black American." They load us with statistics and make assumptions about our situation. The mental capacity of the `black' race is always questioned. The ravages of discrimination, a deficient educational system, and cultural differences are reasons given for explaining our group situation. This endless talk has produced few effective plans for change.

Many Americans of African descent fester in pools of frustration, dismay and failure because they have lost hope. The advancement of others is limited by the system and their fears. Martin Luther King, Malcolm X, Elijah Muhammad, Marcus Garvey and others all had plans to bring equality and dignity to Americans of African ancestry. Each leader created movement toward this goal. Each of them brought hope to the people.

Introduction

Their movements lost momentum after their deaths. The plans of these leaders were either ineffective or unable to function without their strong leadership. Social policies have reversed some gains their leadership brought. Charges of reverse discrimination weakened affirmative action programs. Bakke won a reverse discrimination case against the U.C. DAVIS medical school in 1978. Fights against busing for school integration delayed improved educational opportunity for many students of African descent.

National leadership has been sporadic and confused. Some presidents provided no leadership of their own and often have opposed positive leadership from others. Presidents Reagan and Bush were two national leaders who fought civil rights bills by accusing them of being calls for racial quotas. They had counterparts in the U.S. Congress and on the courts. They didn't use the full force of civil rights laws to fight discrimination against Americans of African ancestry. Sometimes strong laws have been overturned by supreme court decisions.

The lack of effective leadership within the oppressed groups also has been a problem. I do not mean to imply that there is no leadership in the civil rights area. Many are trying to lead. The problem is that these leaders do not present a clear reachable goal. This confuses people. Leaders of factions present conflicting goals with different ideologies. Often they adopt policies that lead nowhere. Some of these policies actual hurt the cause.

First, members of oppressed groups need clearly recognizable goals. It is very important for the group to understand the true goals they are seeking. Next they need possible plans for reaching that goal. They can examine both the goal and the plan. Knowing the goal, everyone can evaluate various plans to see if they lead in the right direction.

Everybody can't lead. But everyone should know the goal. This is the only way they can recognize and avoid those who would lead in the wrong direction. This also increases the number of knowledgeable people creating workable plans.

Many think that by just saying we want "Equality" we have set our goal. If this were true there would be less confusion about plans needed to attain it. No American can argue against the idea of equality. But equality means different things to different people.

Goals

Many Americans want equality for both dark-skinned and pale-skinned citizens, but they want it separately. They would be happy to have completely separate communities for people with different skin color, ancestors or ethnic groups. There are reasons why this will not work.

Since different communities share the one American economy it would be difficult deciding how to share resources. Separate societies and cultures within United States borders are viewed suspiciously. They are subject to harassment and elimination. The destruction of the original native American cultures proves this.

When societies are completely separate, the larger or stronger one will always dominate. Americans of African ancestry or groups with distinctive customs or languages must either be fully integrated into the society, or leave the country completely. If they do not, they will face constant discrimination and harassment. I show ways we can remain and survive in the United States of America, our native land.

There are others seeking not only equality-of-opportunity, but also equality of outcome. Equality-of-outcome guarantees everyone success no matter their effort. Here are examples. Equality of opportunity means that job applicants would be evaluated fairly for employment based on suitable education and job skills. Equality-of-outcome would guarantee high paying jobs for all applicants regardless of qualification. This desire was evident in some plans for attaining equal rights. There is no guarantee of an outcome in a capitalist economy. People seeking it here do not understand the American capitalist system.

Introduction 7

Some people want all the past wrongs corrected so that all groups can start out equally. This is an impossible dream. All people with pale skin didn't profit by the enslavement of Africans. Asking all of them to pay for what some did would be discriminatory. The result of these efforts will be more race hatred and mistrust.

Others wish to ignore all past wrongs and start with a clean slate. This is wrong also. People living today have been and are still victims of discrimination. They are identifiable and should be compensated for the wrongs committed against them.

Many males are fighting for equality between males. They just want to have the same power as the pale-skinned male power elite. Female equality does not interest them. Some people are concerned with equality for just Americans of African ancestry. Others work for the equal treatment of all groups. Others know that the real problem is economic inequality between classes of people. There are many different opinions about equality. Each opinion about equality changes the method of attaining it.

Setting Goals

The Goals of this book are:
1. To establish the following facts in the minds of oppressed groups.
    a. The Fourteenth Amendment to the constitution of the United States of America says you are a citizen because you were born here, or because you were naturalized.
    b. Under the constitution all citizens have the same rights and privileges.
    c. We are full citizens of the United States.
2. To show the need for demanding our full rights as citizens of the United States of American. Demand them not as beggars, but with the dignity and pride of ownership.
3. To reveal the weapons being used to destroy the self image and esteem of Americans of African ancestry.

4. To show errors in thinking that keep oppressed people from taking effective action.
5. To show ways of gaining intellectual, emotional, and moral strength.
6. To show some laws and official practices that protect those who deprive us of portions of our rights and opportunities.
7. To outline the action needed to force national and state governments to investigate and prosecute all businesses, heads of public institutions, law enforcement agencies and individuals that discriminate illegally.

Battle For Control of the Mind

History of Enslavement

America's history of slavery is used to demean American citizens of African ancestry. It is a propaganda weapon used to separate them from other oppressed groups. Others use the history of slavery, as written, to devalue the worth of American citizens of African ancestry. They ask, "How can descendants of slaves be the equal of those of free men? The answers may surprise many Americans. The ancestors of most Americans, of all skin colors, were held in bondage. We will soon see the truth and significance of this.

Most descendants of enslaved kidnaped Africans have wrestled with the issue of slavery. For many the issue remains unresolved and pushed deep into their subconscious. We often talk about it with no outward show of emotion. However, though unspoken and even consciously denied, many of us harbor rage and a sense of shame that our ancestors were enslaved. This rage and shame cause emotional scarring.

I came to grip with derogatory racial remarks early in life and realized the emptiness of their content. They lost their sting. By changing my thinking I denied bigots their control over my emotions. I didn't wait for them to change their attitudes. I seized it. Now racial slurs are like the barking of dogs. The noise warns of possible physical attack, but it transmits no intelligent message.

My reactions to American slavery and the word slave were different. It caused discomfort. I did not handle it well intellectually or emotionally. Then, I still accepted established thinking about slavery. I could not deny the fact of the enslavement. This left me with unflattering conclusions about my African ancestors. Daily experiences confirmed my belief that I was equal to men of any skin color. Still, that history of slavery was very troubling. For years I tried to suppress thoughts of this period. History demanded conclusions I didn't like.

Early in childhood, I read about slavery and was sad. I read the Mandingos and associated series of slave books. Afterwards I avoided this whole subject, because it was so painful. I had no desire to see *Roots* or other modern slave movies. They reminded me of that hated period of slavery and my confused feelings about it. I was puzzled by the pride American citizens of African ancestry claimed from the events shown in the television series. *Roots* was at best a history and geography lesson. It provided a fictionalized history, but could never serve as a symbol of pride for me.

I questioned those who believed otherwise. If I were missing a point, I wanted to find out what it was.

" Why does *Roots* give you pride?" I asked.

"It tells me of my African heritage," was the normal reply.

"But it also shows your ancestors kidnaped and enslaved. It shows your mixed African and European heritage that resulted from the rape of African women. Where is the pride in that?"

This exchange normally made the person I was questioning angry. Some became so angry I feared violence. None of them ever convinced me to take pride in the events shown in *Roots*. Looking back, I think that most of them had been so overwhelmed by negative racial stereotypes that any positive news made them feel good. Just knowing of their ancestors' resistance to slavery made them feel proud. But even this explanation doesn't explain why my questions caused them to become so violently angry. If one has a genuine basis for pride, explaining its basis shouldn't be difficult. Anger seemed an inappropriate response.

Soon I realized the cause for the anger. I understood its message. It showed the deep confused feelings others had about slavery. These people needed something to make themselves feel good about their ancestors and slavery. They took a fictional historical documentary and transformed it into a symbol of racial accomplishment and pride. They were conned or conned themselves into seeing this as a proud moment for the slaves and their descendants. My questions threatened to break the spell. My questions threatened this small respite from slavery's shame.

This showed that others had problems dealing with the idea of their ancestors as slaves. I finally forced myself to face the subject of slavery. In doing so, I realized that what I was trying to deny was shame. I also knew my reactions were irrational. I had to resolve this problem or forever suffer feelings of inferiority.

American literature keeps alive a past relationship between two groups. One group was pale-skinned and free, while the other was dark-skinned and enslaved. Modern literature distorts this past master/slave relationship to transmit a message of superiority and inferiority. These distortions create the impression that aristocratic pale-skinned men dominated stupid, barbaric, dark-skinned people. Every movie, book, or school assignment with a slavery theme repeats this false message of superiority/inferiority.

Pale-skinned Americans try to prove their superiority by tracing their ancestry to a colonist, aristocrat, or free man. Many dark-skinned Americans counter this by ignoring the slavery period. They emphasize the part of their ancestry that included African kings and Egyptian pharaohs. Their facts are true. These history lessons are necessary and very important for the enhancement of their self-esteem. Nevertheless, this tactic does not eliminate the shame they feel for the history of slavery. It fails for two reasons. First, few people are aware of African history. Secondly, the history of African greatness does not eliminate the historical period of slavery.

We must eliminate historical distortions and lies. Then we can evaluate events in their proper setting. Then we can understand their true significance. History shows that the ancestors of Americans from all continents acted in shameful ways. If feeling shame for the acts of one's ancestors is justified, then all Americans

12   Battle for mind Control

should share it. Realistically one should feel neither pride nor shame for actions they didn't contribute to or control.

When American citizens of African ancestry believe the BIG LIE it causes them to have self-image problems. It says that Africans were morally and intellectually inferior to their pale-skinned kidnapers. In truth, all Americans have been duped into revering men with the morals of gangsters. Americans honor outlaws who are falsely characterized as lawful, god fearing men. These men conspired to write immoral laws; they distorted their religious doctrine to justify the kidnaping and enslavement of citizens from another country.

African citizens who were kidnaped and brought here were not slaves. They were free African citizens. One would have expected America's Christian citizens to rescue them and prosecute their captors. Arrest and punishment should have been assured for the outlaws. This didn't happen. America's political, legal and economic leaders joined in a conspiracy with the kidnappers. When I say kidnappers, I include the European, American and African conspirators. I also refer to the American business community that enslaved the kidnaped victims. Most damning of all, I also refer to the clergy who distorted biblical text to justify the Africans' enslavement.

Kidnappers weren't prosecuted because their activities were legalized. Profits from their barbaric acts encouraged them to continue. American agents housed the kidnaped victims until they could sell them into slavery. American merchants and plantation owners profited by forcing the Africans to work without pay.

Many kidnaped African females were raped by their captors. Children created from these rapes, the kidnapers own children, worked as slaves. Historians show African women as willing lovers with their captors. This is a rapist's fantasy. Captive people can neither give nor withhold consent. They can only react to force. Rape!

The kidnapers called their victims slaves. Then they falsely named themselves as their owners and masters. This was self-

Battle for mind Control

serving, because criminal acts never give kidnapers the right to own their victims. It's important to understand the significance of this simple fact. One should read and think about it until they understand its significance. Do not think of the Africans as dark-skinned slaves of pale-skinned masters. Think of them as kidnaped people forced to work as slaves. It may seem a small difference, but you will come to understand that there is a very important distinction being made.

Since the criminals wrote history, we have their version of it. They show a false master over slave relationship, instead of the crime of criminal exploiting victims. Civilized people do not use skin color differences as justification for kidnaping and enslaving foreign citizens. Civilized people do not legalize kidnappers ownership rights to their victims.

By calling their victims slaves, the kidnappers moved to destroy images of them as free citizens worthy of being rescued. They wanted to conceal their history as free African people. People with a history have rights. America blocked the Africans' path to freedom when it legalized the kidnappers false labels of master and slave.

When we think of the Africans only as slaves, it is natural to accept them being owned by a master. But, when we think of the Africans properly as kidnaped victims, it logically follows that their kidnappers were criminals. When one uses accurate facts in their thinking process, they see the significance of certain historical acts differently. Here it is clear that the European and American business people acted in uncivilized ways.

Confuse and distort the way people think and you have prepared them to accept deception. They will believe lies and distortions even when it opposes logic. America's ruling male minority has taught most Americans to think in distorted ways. That is why they believe the lies about slavery and tolerate the oppression of their fellow citizens. America's school system distorts thinking by teaching inaccurate history. Suddenly the victims, law abiding Africans, change to slaves. Criminal kidnaping conspirators

14 Battle for mind Control

are recast as respectable law abiding businessmen. Americans turn deaf ears to screaming historical facts telling them this version is wrong. Oppressed Americans have all the facts needed to build a strong self-image. First we must discard old distorted beliefs. Then we must learn how to think differently. After reevaluating historical events, we will recognize the falseness of things long accepted as true. I suggest that you begin practicing a changed way of thinking by immediately rereading the previous three paragraphs. See history from a different perspective.

Remember,
"Africans who were brought here in chains, were not slaves. They were free African citizens who had been kidnaped. Their kidnapers were criminals."

What significance do these facts have for you as an American?
1. Do they make you feel better or worse about your ancestors?
2. Do they make you feel better or worse about yourself?
3. Do they change the way you look at the moral standards of African people? European people?
4. Do they make you disbelieve the moral superiority claimed by European people?
5. Do they show the danger of basing one's self-image on the reported acts of ancestors?

This example shows how shifting the point of view alters our evaluation of historical events. Other examples will help change the way you see yourself. You'll see how faulty thinking distorts your self-image. With practice you will come to see historical facts differently. This will show that you are changing and improving the way you think.

America used another form of limited bondage before it turned to kidnaping Africans. They had indentured servants.

Battle for mind Control 15

Indentured servants were people working in bondage to pay off debts. When the debt was worked off, they were freed. Wealthy colonist looked for ways to increase their wealth. They decided it would be more profitable to enslave people for life and not just for periods needed to pay off debt.

There were several reasons Europeans decided to kidnap Africans. First, African nations were not strong enough to protect their citizens from the kidnappers. Secondly, skin color and religious differences made it easier to justify enslaving Africans. Colonial rulers passed laws denying Africans their freedom after their bondage as indentured servitude. Free Africans living in America were not enslaved. But their rights were severely limited. I will not go into great detail about this period, because good history books cover it well.[1]

Some African nations also enslaved people and were slavers. Many people devalue all African cultures because some worked the slave trade. This is another example of distorted thinking. Each African culture should be evaluated on its own merits. If blanket continental blame were appropriate, all European nations would share the blame for Hitler's and Stalin's atrocities.

It's difficult for good citizens to control the actions of a criminal element intent on breaking the law. The American legal system could not stop alcohol sales during prohibition. It seems powerless to stop drug smuggling. Thousands of American children are reported missing every year. Many are kidnaped and enslaved in sexual exploitation schemes. Some are even taken out of the country. Americans don't consider their culture depraved because some of its citizens are outlaws.

Moralists fault African nations because they failed to protect their citizens from European kidnaping raids. Many American citizens of African ancestry personalize this shame and feel inferior to Europeans. The United States of America is the most powerful country in the world. Yet, it has been unable to prevent the kidnaping of some of its educated and influential citizens.

During the seventies and eighties, terrorist groups frequently kidnaped Americans and held them as hostages. Our military could not even rescue its soldiers from years of imprisonment in Korea and Viet Nam. Some were enslaved. Americans were angry and frustrated about the taking of hostages. But, none felt inferior to those foreign cultures that condoned the kidnaping of free citizens from America. We do not believe the laws of other countries make American hostages into slaves. The kidnappers can call them criminals, prisoners of war, war criminals or slaves, but they are still kidnaped victims to us.

African nations were as powerless against European kidnappers as are civilized societies against today's terrorists. While Europeans were kidnaping Africans, non-Christian nations were kidnaping and enslaving Europeans. They were doing so with the help of European outlaws.[2] The scale of kidnaping from Europe was not as great, but it did exist.

As recently as the second world war, Japan kidnaped and enslaved hundreds of thousands of American, Korean, Filipino and Chinese men and women. Germany did the same to millions of Europeans. After the war, they were freed. Since they lost the war, Japan and Germany could not pass self-serving laws making their captives legal slaves. Expressing a notion that the Germans and Japanese were the masters and owners of the people they had enslaved would have been considered absurd. Instead, other nations were shocked by their barbarous acts. Americans, Koreans, Filipinos and Chinese were not devalued because of their victimization. The Germans and Japanese were not honored for their shameful acts.

Clear thinking people will judge all kidnaping and enslavement the same. We also must brand the European and American acts of kidnaping and enslavement as immoral and barbaric. A group indulges in fantasy when they assume an air of superiority based on their ancestors criminal acts. The opposite is true. Obviously it's fantasy that the criminal acts of some Europeans made them morally superior to Africans. This is another place where we must discard old distorted ways of thinking. Thinking clearly, we will feel the same revulsion toward the criminals in America's history that we feel for German and Japanese criminals.

European Slaves

The idea of enslaving people was not new to Europeans. Europe's ruling classes had forced their peasants into servitude for centuries. The peasant serfs were legally parts of the land. Their children were born into this unfree status. During Europe's feudal period, there was a shortage of workers. Peasants often moved from one estate to another to improve their living conditions. The ruling land owners did not like this. They wanted more control over their peasant workers. Kings wanted to be sure that the noblemen made money so they could pay taxes. So, the various European countries passed laws that bound the peasants to the lands they worked.

Europeans have always argued that serfs were not slaves. Compare the dictionary definition of slavery with the life of the serfs and then decide if you believe they were slaves.

SLAVE:
1. **A person held in servitude as the chattel of another: Bondsman**
2. **A person who has lost control of himself and is dominated by something or someone.**

(*Webster's Seventh New Collegiate Dictionary* 1972)

Serfs became a part of the noble landlord's estate. They had to work on it and could not legally leave it. Like the enslaved Africans in America, serfs who left the land were hunted down, forced to return and punished. A 1500 Prussian law set the following punishment for a runaway serf. Nail him to a post by his ear. Give him a knife to cut himself free [3] Succeeding generations were born into bondage as serfs. So, like the children of kidnaped

Africans, European children were born into bondage. When the lord sold portions of his estate, he sold the serfs along with it. Historians insist that the serfs were not slaves because they had certain protected rights. They would not call them slaves; they called them unfree persons. It is true that the serfs had certain protected rights. The same lord or nobleman who owned them as serfs also had the duty to protect the serfs' rights. It other words, he protected the serfs from himself. In some circumstances the king might intercede for the rights of the serfs.

Today, powerful men rarely oppose each other to protect the rights of workers or the poor. Bankers show more concern for corporate profits than they do for the condition of workers. Powerful politicians don't side with low income neighborhoods against large polluting refineries or factories. It was less common for powerful men to do so during the middle ages. The king acted to guarantee his tax collections. Mostly he sided with the nobles who needed income to pay his tax. Serf labor provided this income. One can be sure he sided with the landlord so as not to jeopardize income.

Serfs farmed sections of the estate for themselves. The landlord assigned each serf a small strip of land from his estate. Serfs used the land, but they did not receive ownership rights. They only had the right to use it to support themselves. Landlords didn't feed or support serfs so they had to provide them some means for self support. This was a poor exchange for their freedom.

Serfs received no pay for working the landlord's portion of the estate. Normally serfs worked at least three days a week for the landlord. The landlord could demand extra labor from the serfs if his needs increased. Sometimes he worked them six days a week. Landlords used the serfs as free labor to grow and market their crops. They often took portions of serfs' crops. They also used them for building roads, manor repairs and completing other required tasks.

Serf marriages also were controlled by the landlord. He was the only one who could grant them permission to marry off the

Battle for mind Control

estate. He demanded pay for his consent. This was his way of getting paid for a lost worker. In principle he sold the serf to the other estate. When a serf died, the landlord took his most prized livestock and other valuable possessions. The serf's family got what was left. There were differences between the life of kidnaped Africans in America and Europe's serfs. My point is that there were many likenesses.

The definition of slavery is not based on the rights others allow you to have. It is based on whether you have the legal freedom of your person. That is whether you are owned by someone else. The serfs were legally controlled and owned by others. Their children were born into bondage. Ownership of them was exchanged between nobles. If serfdom was not slavery, it was its ugly twin.

Everyone knows that slavery existed in America until 1865. History books, movies and television stories never let us forget it. They down play the similar slave conditions many European peasants endured at the same time. Russian serfs were not freed until 1860, just four years before American slavery ended. During the sixteenth and seventeenth centuries Russian peasants were transformed from free peasants to unfree serfs. Nine-tenths of the Russian people were peasants and by 1678 over 70 percent of them were unfree serfs. By the 1700s they had even lost their legal tie to the land. They were slaves. Russian noblemen sold them on the auction block as chattel. Serfs were cruelly disciplined by whipping. Families were broken up, usually by selling off the children.[4]

American Slavery/ European Serfdom

1. Both were born into bondage.
2. Both were sold by others.
3. Both forced by law to work for others without pay.
4. Both subjected to physical punishment by the landowner.

5. Both gained freedom by buying it from the landowner or by government decree.
6. Americans kidnaped and enslaved Africans.
7. Europeans put their own peasants in bondage.

Some text books now acknowledge that both were forms of slavery. Most Europeans and their American descendants play word games to conceal the obvious. Ruling classes in European nations bought and sold their peasants. Whether one calls them slaves or serfs they were unfree. Since 80% to 90% of the European peasants were serfs during the feudal period, the ancestors of most Europeans were serfs. Landlords held European peasant serfs in bondage; they also were unfree. One needs to use these facts to make an important change in thinking.

American citizens of African ancestry are not the only ones whose ancestors worked as unfree labor. If ancestor bondage is a cause for shame, European descendants also should feel shame. Both groups should feel shame for the bondage of their ancestors, or neither group should.

This is a very important point for American citizens of African ancestry to realize. American citizens of European ancestry also descend from slaves. The mind needs time to adjust to a new idea. Keep them fresh in your mind and eventually they will replace the erroneous beliefs you held for a lifetime.

Of what significance are these facts? Each individual must make their own decision.

1. If these facts are new to you, does it change the way you feel about yourself or others?
2. If you already knew them, will you now analyze them differently and change the way you compare people?
3. Do you now feel differently about your African and/or European ancestors? Do you still feel the same level of pride or shame about them?
4. How does this affect your self-image?

5. Should the actions of ancestors affect your self-esteem? If so, why and how much should it influence your feelings about yourself?
6. What do you think rulers consider when they pass laws that enslave people?

Obviously some Americans can claim that they descend from Europe's ruling classes and not peasants. American citizens of African ancestry can make the same claim. Free Africans lived in America before its period of slavery. They lived here before America's ruling class conspired to enslave Africans. They and their descendants mostly remained free.

Nevertheless, it would be unreasonable for either group to make this claim. Today's rich and powerful European landowners are the most likely descendants of the freemen of the middle ages. Few of them would have left positions of power and wealth for life in colonial America. Also, most darker skinned Americans are descendants of enslaved Africans. Individual situations are not important. The main point is that bondage was common for the ancestors of both groups.

How could people fail for centuries to see that serfs were the same as slaves? How could the ruling class get around the church's prohibition against enslaving Christians?

1. First they labeled the peasants as unfree peasant serfs instead of slaves. They justified the distinction by making some differences between the lives of serfs and those they called slaves.
2. Next, they emphasized the fact that serfs were bound to the land and not the landlord.
3. Then, they ignored the fact that runaway serfs were hunted down, returned and brutally punished just as a slave would be.
4. Fourth, they ignored the fact that children born to serfs were owned and controlled by the lords, the same as slaves.

5. Finally, they emphasized the differences between the unfree states of serfs and slaves and ignored the similarities. This allowed them falsely to claim that they were not enslaving their pale-skinned Christian peasants.

Peasants had no choice in entering the unfree status. No one wants to believe their lot is the lowest. Serfs wanted to believe they were in a category above slaves. Their descendants have the same delusion. Educated Americans and Europeans have always known these facts. They deny the obvious because it threatens their self-image.

Many American citizens of African ancestry also know these historical facts. But they also argue that the serf's bondage was different and not real slavery. A lifetime of indoctrination distorts their thinking. They look up to their oppressor and down on themselves. Their mind molds can only cast superior pale-skinned images and inferior dark-skinned ones. Their minds reject facts that do not fit this mold. We must destroy these molds. We need minds that can form fresh new ideas and methods for fighting oppression.

Europeans as Morally Superior

Most people accept the idea of America as being founded on strong moral principles and religious values. However, one doubts the sincerity of people's moral values who systematically massacred the native American population. Belief in their moral values is completely destroyed when one learns how their government conspired to kidnap and enslave foreigners.

There is another obvious instance of Christians twisting their religious teaching to justify immoral acts. Religious leaders condemned Africans as pagans. Within their logic this justified kidnaping and enslaving Africans. These religious leaders blessed the slavers and said they served God by bringing pagan Africans to Christian America. In America, claimed the religious leaders, Africans would be converted to Christianity. Then they made it illegal to teach Christianity to Africans. Even when they converted to Christianity, Africans were not freed. Religious leaders decreed that it was still moral to enslave Christians, if they were black. A 1667 Virginia law had this line, "The conferring of baptisme doth not alter the condition of the person as to his bondage or freedom."[5] Some slave holders had their slaves attend church with them. There, slaves heard sermons telling them to obey their masters and wait for their salvation in heaven.

They helped in creating a wall of hate between the races. Much of that hate exists today. In fairness, I must acknowledge that later more enlightened religious leaders fought for the abolition of slavery. However, most of America's leaders must have been immoral for slavery to have lasted so long.

People excuse them by saying that they were just men of their times. I don't deny that they were. I only say that they lacked praiseworthy morals. The morals of the day were self-serving. Great leaders are people who rise above the limited thinking of their time. An enlightened Malcolm X was such a man. His principles expressed a love for all men. He did so during a time of intense racial violence. He renounced racial hatred when he could have gained power by continuing to embrace it. Petty leaders accept self- aggrandizement and selfishly promote policies that enrich them at others' expense. Many of America's early leaders, as men of their times, fall into this category.

Many will point to the brilliance of these men in laying the foundations for our government. They would be right. I am not denying that these were highly educated men. I say that they were immoral men. They set up a system designed to meet only their needs. The new government had many benefits for its citizens. But the benefits were restricted to wealthy pale-skinned males. The poor, Africans and even their own women were excluded from the benefits of this government. They were above average men in their accomplishments, but not in moral integrity.

Pale-skinned American women fared little better than Africans. None could vote. If married, they were totally under the control of their husbands. They didn't even have the legal right to the custody of their children or land. Their husbands had the legal right to whip them. More than a hundred years passed before women even received the right to vote in 1920.

Supreme Court Justice Brennan argued that protectionist laws in practical effect, put women, not on a pedestal, but in a cage . . . Throughout much of the 19th century the position of women was, in many respects, comparable to that of blacks under the pre-Civil War slave codes. Neither slaves nor women could hold office, serve on juries, or bring suit in their own names, and married women were denied the legal capacity to hold or convey property or to serve as legal guardians for their own children. (Frontier v Richardson, 411 U.S.677 (1973)

Women still suffer brutal beatings by their husbands. Normal laws of assault and battery do not protect them because the law categorizes them differently. Only recently has wife beating become a crime. Victims still have great difficulty prosecuting rapists. Today's women have difficulty getting legal protection from physical, sexual and emotional abuse. Can you imagine the abuse they suffered when only powerful pale-skinned men had legal rights?

Close comparisons show a likeness between those men and modern crime syndicates, high level drug pushers and pimps. They lived grandly, supported by the brutal physical and emotional exploitation of others.

The shame of these men's actions extend beyond their emotional and physical abuse of kidnaped Africans. It even extends past the exploitation of their own mothers and sisters. As the educated religious ruling class, they should have set the standards for fairness and morality. But yielding to greed, they distorted religious doctrine and promoted racial hatred to simplify worker exploitation. American society still suffers from their acts.

Is there a greater unifying force then a common belief in a divine power or rational principles of ethics? I think not. A country founded on religious principles should reflect this. Instead, the founding fathers have robbed Americans of the beauty of this spiritual oneness. A campaign of racial hatred, while useful in furthering their economic goals, built divisiveness and intolerance into our social institutions.

A person's skin color or ethnic group is more meaningful as measures of human worth in America than adherence to moral or ethical standards. Many Americans more readily identify with criminals who have a similar skin color than they do with other law abiding citizens with a different skin color. Even common religious beliefs take a back seat to skin color considerations. This is a sad testimony for a nation built on religious principles. Relations are improving. However, the country is still paying for centuries of immoral leadership.

Kidnaped Africans and their descendants are not the only citizens paying for the greed of those evil men. False indoctrination also jeopardizes the well being of their own descendants. As a result, many of them are full of mistrust and hate for all people who have color in their skin. Even those who do not hate, believe many negative stereotypes about dark-skinned individuals. They become victims of the hatred they adopted. Since hate and love cannot exist together, they doom themselves. None can ever know the joy of spiritual fellowship with fellow humans.

The moral corruption so evident at all levels of our political, educational and commercial institutions reflect this spiritual emptiness. Hate and suspicion contaminates those people and institutions that hold them. It is surely evident that something is contaminating the spiritual fiber of America's social and family structures.

History shows that the moral fiber of early America was shallow or nonexistent. Even their own distorted historical accounts can't cloak their immorality. No group need feel inferior to the standards set by these men.

I make no claim that the Africans were morally superior to early European settlers. I have no research to back such a claim.

Making claims of African cultural superiority would be just as foolish as one for European superiority. It's safe to say that people in Africa were at least the moral equals of people in Europe.

American citizens of African ancestry have no reason to feel morally inferior to others. Take time to review the facts presented here. Use them to create new ideas about people. I remind you that new patterns of thinking take time and practice. It will take time for these facts to sink in and become real to you. When they have, your feelings that dark-skinned Americans are morally inferior to pale-skinned people should fade away. If they do not, then have the following mental discussion with yourself or with others.

(I know that the kidnappers and their society were immoral. What has happened since then to prove that the moral standards of pale-skinned people are superior to mine?)

You know you have improved your thinking techniques when you can understand the significance of these truths. It is a first step in eliminating faulty thinking that destroys self-esteem. The BIG lie is ineffective when confronted with facts and sound reasoning. Still, one must work at developing sound reasoning techniques. If you do not, you will continue to hold beliefs that make you feel inferior. Others are sure to treat you no better than you feel you should be treated.

> **If one believes they are inferior, they will adopt inferior thoughts and attitudes. Their actions will reflect their low self-esteem. They will make themselves inferior.**

Many well educated minds come in brown-skinned bodies. Some of these individuals have gained great material wealth. Many also still conceal feelings of inferiority. Their state of mind is revealed in panels and talk shows about race relations. They frantically defend the mythical black race against a pale-skinned speaker's accusations. It's as though they seek validation for the right to exist as a United States citizen.

Sometimes the person from the oppressed group responds with verbal attacks against the pale-skinned group. Their methods of attack often reveal their inferior defensive attitude. They attack the whole group instead of directing their attacks against those who practice oppression. When they do this, they commit two grave errors.

First, they should challenge individual's statements or activities. They should not make verbal attacks based on skin color or ethnic identification. When they use racial attacks to counter racial bigotry they make it a more powerful weapon for oppression. One loses the power struggle when they play by their opponent's rules and into their strengths. Members of the ruling elite use negative racial and gender stereotypes expertly as weapons of oppression. Any appeal to racial bigotry increases their power.

When one attacks another because of their skin color, they validate oppression based on skin colors. Negative stereotypes about dark-skinned people are more common than those about pale-skinned people. So, those with darker skin colors are at a disadvantage in using skin color as a weapon. Fighting oppression with the truth has more positive effects. Truth about individuals and groups decreases the usefulness of racial and sexual bigotry as weapons.

It may seem as though I engage in racial attacks when I speak of a powerful pale-skinned male group. This is not so. A small group of pale-skinned men have been America's ruling elite for centuries. Although most can't see it, pale-skinned men and women of the working classes also are exploited. Even when speaking against the ruling elites, I am not attacking their skin color. I only attack their methods of using racial and sexual oppression for financial gain.

Here is an example where responding to bigoted racial attacks in the wrong way, increases their harm.

(Moderator)	Black people rioted and looted stores during the 1992 Los Angeles riots. This shows that black Americans don't have the work ethic or the high moral standards of Koreans. Black people are more likely to commit crimes. Why aren't black people law abiding and industrious like Koreans?
(Panelist)	It's not fair to compare Koreans with black Americans. We've known centuries of oppression and discrimination. The unemployment rate among black Americans, in Los Angeles is high. These people were just getting some basic items they needed to survive.

In answering the moderator's charges this way, the panelist not only acknowledged their truth, but also showed feelings of inferiority. The panelist failed to challenge the moderator's implication that individual acts show group values. This gives in to racial stereotyping. This hypothetical scene reenacts many live ones I've witnessed. Here is a better response.

(Moderator)	Black people rioted and looted stores during the 1992 Los Angeles riots. This proves that black Americans don't have the work ethic or the high moral standards of Koreans. Black people are more likely to commit crimes. Why aren't black people law abiding and industrious like Koreans?
(Panelist)	Your assumptions are wrong. Not all Los Angeles citizens took part in the riots. All brown-skinned people can't be branded for the actions of rioters. Rioters were a small part of the population. Their actions do not show group morals. Also, people of various skin colors, nationalities and ethnic groups took part in the riots. Television cameras showed pale-skinned people, along with people of Mexican and Asian descent taking part in the looting. Why are you singling out one group for condemnation?

Battle for mind Control

(Moderator)   Black people started this riot, and usually are involved in more riots than other groups.

(Panelist)   How do you know this? Where do you get your facts?

(Moderator)   The whole nation could see it on television. We saw the riot begin at the intersection in the black neighborhood when black people started assaulting passing motorists.

(Panelist)   Was this the first place the riot started or just the first place television recorded it? Television coverage is selective because there are a limited number of cameras. They were looking for trouble in certain areas, so this is what they covered. Television didn't cover the Los Angeles riots. They mainly only covered one group's role in the riots. Social evaluations can't be made from unbalanced television coverage.

I'll end the exchange here. Compare the two exchanges.

The second exchange shows how one arrives at different conclusions when they aren't hindered by false assumptions.

DON'T BE IN SUCH A HURRY TO DEFEND YOURSELF OR YOUR GROUP THAT YOU FAIL TO ANALYZE THE QUESTION.

You must be sure that you and the speaker don't have hidden biases. You should always look for false assumptions in your own thinking and in the statements of others. I pointed out some false assumptions that the moderator made. There are a combination of at least ten false assumptions and false conclusions in the moderator's statements. How many can you identify?

We must seek out and destroy all the hidden stereotypes we believe about ourselves. This can only happen if we learn how to change our thinking. We must replace thoughts of failure and incompetence with those of confidence and pride. With our pride and self-esteem intact, we can fight and overcome all the other seemingly insurmountable problems. Developing an understanding of the way historical distortions destroy peoples self-image is a good starting point.

Thinking

The most difficult battle in the world, is to change faulty thinking patterns. First, we must recognize the need to change. Then we must seek out new truths. Lastly, we must adopt these truths and make them the basis for a new philosophy. Each step is difficult, because doubt, laziness and force of habit, continually pull us back to old thinking patterns and beliefs. But with persistence, the changes become permanent. Make the changes and know the richness in life that clear thinking will bring. Otherwise, you will forever know the pain of shame, doubt and inferiority.

African-Americans

So now you're calling yourself an African-American. You say you're proud to be African-American. Why? If you respond to this question like most people, your answer will be vague and confused. The usual answer is, "Because my ancestors came from Africa." When I ask why this makes them an African-American, they mumble something about being proud to be the descendant of the great kings of Africa. If challenged further, many become defensive and hostile. Why the hostility?

The questions make them uneasy, because they are not comfortable with their newly assumed identity. Changing labels doesn't necessarily change the person. When they adopt the label of African-American, people set themselves up for the greatest ego deflating trip imaginable.

Americans whose ancestors came from Africa have an identity crisis. They have a problem about what other Americans will call them. However, the biggest crisis is within their own minds. People have image problems when they identify themselves with fuzzy imprecise labels. Voluntarily adopting the identity of African-Americans is an image destroying act.

When I've questioned the wisdom of using the African-American label, I've been verbally attacked as having a `white' man's attitude. For the record, I have a dark skin color and definitely have African ancestors. This doesn't make me proud or ashamed. These are just facts of my existence.

Those encouraging us to call ourselves African-Americans say we need to do so to build our self-esteem. They believe we need a separate identity from Americans with pale skin. Their thinking is confused.

There are American citizens of African ancestry living in the USA. This means that some of their ancestors lived in Africa. This is different from being an African living in America (African-American). Many pale-skinned people also have African ancestors.

They will deny it. If African ancestry is the basis for being African-American, they are African-American also.

You can never build true self-esteem from a distorted self-image. Assuming a false identity as African-American is a futile attempt to do so. This label doesn't describe an existing cultural group. It's an attempt to create the idea of such a group in the minds of Americans. It's an inadequate mechanism for building self-esteem that will fail. Ultimately, it will cause more damage than good.

Children from the group calling themselves African-Americans will experience an identity crisis and damaged esteem. These children will be worse off than the miserable lost souls of today. They'll be foreigners in their native land. They will have a functional knowledge of neither African nor American cultures. Their leaders will have trapped them in a false culture. Americans of African ancestry must learn that the adoption of a label won't create self-esteem.

Advantages can come from adopting a new personal or group identity. There are historical and biblical examples of individual and group name changes. Identity changes are worthwhile when the old identity is a false one imposed by others. Rejecting the "Negro" label was such a positive move.

It was more accurate to describe the two groups as `black' and `white' and not as `white' and "the Negro." Black and white are at least attempts at describing physical features. These are false descriptions also. Using them causes a different set of problems.

"Dark-skinned" and "pale-skinned" persons would be more descriptive. Negro was the name used by people from Europe to describe us. Parents name their children. Owners name their possessions. When we allowed them to create our label, we allowed them to believe that they created and owned us.

When Americans of African ancestry rejected the label of Negro, they also rejected the paternalistic attitudes of pale-skinned Americans. Actually, the situation was reversed. The group had a change in self-awareness, then they changed the group label. In the fifties and sixties, Americans of African ancestry came to see

African-Americans   33

themselves in a different light. The changed awareness then caused them to reject the previous label of Negro.

But there are many reasons why adopting the label of African-American is a destructive move. I'll detail some of them to show why it's not the best action for oppressed people to take. You'll understand why the African-American label hinders instead of helps our quest for full citizenship in our native country.

First, it's a false identity. African-American suggests a recent immigrant. If it doesn't suggest a recent immigrant, then it suggests the first or second generation of an immigrant family.

People calling themselves African-Americans are not recent immigrants. African ancestors of most Americans arrived here centuries ago. They became citizens by passage of the Thirteenth and Fourteenth amendments. The fourteenth amendment was adopted in 1868. So most of our families have been here for many generations.

African-American could apply to people who have migrated to this country, but have retained their unique physical characteristics, their language or their ancestral culture. Does the African-American group qualify as a racial or ethnic group based on these standards? I don't think that they can.

Is a person an African-American because of skin color? If so what skin color do they have? People usually use the terms `black' and African-American synonymously. Does this mean that African-Americans all have black skin? This is doubtful, because few, if any, Americans have truly black skin. Are all African-Americans dark brown? Can African-Americans have tan or cream colored skin? Is there a paleness limit for African-American skin color? Except mythical blackness, African-Americans have no particular skin color.

Do African-Americans claim other distinct physical characteristics. Is kinky hair texture a characteristic that African-Americans have? Can a person with straight hair still be an African-American? What other distinctive physical features must one have to be called African-American? To my knowledge, people don't have to look a certain way to qualify as African-Americans.

African-Americans

Is having an African ancestor the only qualification one needs to be an African-American? Must one have an unbroken line of African ancestors to qualify as an African-American? If not, how many ancestors from other continents can one have and still identify themselves as African-American? Will having one distant African ancestor followed by generations of European, Asian or indigenous American ancestors qualify one as African-American?

If African-Americans do not restrict their gene pool, they can't claim to have inherited specific African physical characteristics. This would mean that there is no specific way for an African-American to look or act based on physically inherited characteristics. So there is no sound claim for the label here.

Next, few Americans of African ancestry have any cultural knowledge of their ancestral homeland. Language, social customs, religion and traditional forms of earning a living are the foundation of any culture. Let's see how the African-American group fits into this description.

Few persons in the group calling themselves African-American know anything about Africa. Many don't even realize that Africa is a continent and not a country. They don't realize that there are many different nations on the African continent. There are more than thirty nations on the continent of Africa. They would be even more surprised if they knew the diversity of African physical features. The inhabitants of some African nations don't have the traditional dark skin or kinky hair normally associated with Africa.

Since they don't know the geography of Africa, it would be difficult for African-Americans to know what section of Africa their ancestors came from. There are estimated to be three thousand ethnic groups living in Africa.

Ties with their ancestral home would come through family cultural traditions. Families could have passed African cultural information down through the generations. This hasn't happened. Few American families can boast of practicing African culture and custom as a family tradition.

Few "African-Americans" know anything about African cultural practices. That is why they are trying to identify with a

African-Americans 35

whole continent, instead of a cultural group on that continent. This would be the same as assuming you were Chinese just because your ancestors came from Asia.

Those claiming to be African-Americans don't speak an African language. Language is a basic feature of a culture. Speaking the language is basic for inclusion in the culture. Fifty basic languages and thousands of dialects are spoken in Africa. There are no written forms for most of these dialects. So, unless the language comes down through the generations, Americans have no way of knowing their ancestral language.

Americans of African ancestry don't even speak a modern African language or dialect as a second language. This makes it extremely difficult to maintain the customs and culture of their ancestors. So "African-Americans" can't claim language as a cultural base.

Many speakers and authors claim a `black' language. I know of no such language. To what do they refer? What language do they claim? They refer to certain word patterns or inflections that they claim are unique to persons of African ancestry. Even if this were true, it hardly forms the basis for claims to a language.

American children imitate area speech patterns. Southerners of all skin colors have speech patterns more in common with each other, than other persons of similar color in other parts of the country. This also is true of persons from the Northeast and western parts of the country. So the speech patterns of children of African descent are more influenced by their American social environment than by their African culture heritage.

African-Americans do not follow African religious rituals, so spiritual they are not African. Religion plays a major role in the culture of a nation or people. Religion was particularly significant in the daily lives of Africans. This is different from many western religions that separate religion from routine daily activities.

Some African people adopted Christianity centuries ago. But it wasn't the religion of the kidnaped Africans. Most African-Americans now accept Christianity as their religion. They neither practice nor understand the religion of their African ancestors. The fact that the Africans were not Christian was the justification Europeans used to kidnap and enslave them.

Christianity influences American culture. It even affects the lives of people of other religions. Whether Jewish, Moslem, Hindu or other religious worshiper, all Americans observe many Christian holidays and religious standards. So in the area of religion, African-Americans are culturally more Christian and American than they are African.

African-Americans can't claim a unique way of earning a living for a cultural base. They have no special job skills, or trades traceable to Africa. So, they cannot claim this category as one that gives them a distinctive cultural characteristic.

People adopting the African-American label will say that these things aren't important. They claim people can educate themselves about African cultural practices. I agree. Classes about African cultures can and should be taken. One's education is incomplete without knowledge of Africa and its people.

I don't agree that book learning can transform you from American into the particular African culture studied. How is learning about a distant culture going to change a person's everyday culture? Learning about other cultures and adopting some of their ways will change a person. However, it won't make them like those of the studied culture. At best it'll make them a blend of the new culture and their own.

What is the difference between an American with dark skin and one with pale skin learning about Africa? Why would it make one an African-American and not the other? Americans with African ancestors might have a more personal relationship with the material, but this wouldn't make them African-Americans.

Cultural identity comes from inherited customs and values, not pure book learning. Life long experiences contribute to cultural awareness. People are easier to understand when you study their culture. But study doesn't create the experience of living in that culture. Without these experiences you can't fully understand their beliefs or duplicate their thinking patterns.

African-Americans

Defenders of African-Americanism may disagree with me. They may concede ground and acknowledge that book learning would not make them Africans. However, they could argue that the African-American label shows the dual cultural influence in their lives. They may also say that their ancestral genes make them both African and American.

These are weak arguments. "African-Americans" have wide ranges of skin coloring. Those with lighter have genetic input from Asia and Europe. Estimates claim that 20 to 75 percent of people labeled as `black' also have European ancestors.[6]

An accurate label reflecting ancestry would be African-European-American. You can't ignore major parts of your ancestry if you wish to show your true heritage. African-American claimants would argue that the American in their African-American label shows the European influence. To accept this argument I would have to believe that only the pale-skinned descendants of Europeans can be real Americans. This I am not prepared to do.

So, what are the consequences of claiming false or imprecise identities? Feelings of inadequacy, a confused self-image, and lack of direction are some consequences of claiming false labels. It definitely sets the group up for ridicule. How can a people really feel good about themselves, when their identity is a fabrication.

Many people become hostile when questioned about the legitimacy of identifying themselves as African-Americans. Subconsciously they already know that there is little foundation for adopting this label. Many use this new label as the In-thing to do. Others use it because they desperately search for anything that will make them feel better about themselves. They search for a label that will make them feel better about the plight of their oppressed group. Instead, what results are more feelings of inadequacy.

Having insufficient knowledge about Africa, the place they claim for a cultural base, causes feelings of inadequacy. Guilt weights on them for not spending more time learning about African ways. They feel like impostors, because their real values are American and not with those they believe Africans should have.

"You know your heritage, because they teach it in school. We don't know who we are, because the white man robbed the black man of his heritage when he brought him to this country."

I've overheard conversations like this several times on California college campuses. Students from eastern colleges have expressed similar opinions. I'm sure it's repeated on campuses throughout the country. It makes me sad when I hear intelligent young Americans express such confused thinking.

First they mistakenly accept school book history as accurate history. Next, with no supporting facts, they believe they are culturally different from other Americans. They see skin color differences and assume cultural differences. I don't see how people can conclude they're culturally different without knowing the traits that make them different. They've accepted African-American as the title for the `black' culture they can't define.

We expect people claiming membership in a cultural group to be able to express its traits. Their actions and beliefs should differ from ours. They should have knowledge of that culture that we lack. They disappoint us when they can't speak the language, or don't know anything special about the claimed culture. We feel their claim is false.

Lacking this ability, people make excuses. My parents didn't teach me the language. Or we no longer follow those customs. What they really are saying is that culturally they are different from their ancestors. Individuals who identify themselves as African-Americans will find themselves in the same situation.

Whenever schools, or cities have cultural day, Americans of African descent feel obligated to assume Africa as their cultural base. Why? They don't know anything about Africa. Ask them to name two modern African nations and show where to find them on the African continent. Few could do so. Question them about the leadership of at least two African nations. Challenge them to speak

African-Americans

some African words, describe an African religion, or name an African god. Ask them to tell you some traditional African names or sing one African song. Fewer than 2 percent of those persons claiming to be African-Americans could correctly answer any of those questions.

This movement to call Americans of African ancestry African-Americans is supposed to build self-esteem. Instead, it is a time bomb that will destroy the self-esteem of those who adopt it. Any positive gains will be fleeting.

Picture the following scene.

Brown-skinned Afram and pale-skinned Charles are eating lunch in a school cafeteria.

(Charles)	Things are bad in other countries. I'm glad I'm an American. How about you?
(Afram)	I'm African-American.
(Charles)	Really! How long've you been here?
(Afram)	All my life, I was born here.
(Charles)	Oh? . . . . When did your parents get here?
(Afram)	They were born here, just like yours.
(Charles)	Then why do you call yourself African-American and not American?
(Afram)	(with pride) Because all black people came from Africa.
(Charles)	What part of Africa did you come from?
(Afram)	I don't know. South Africa I think.
(Charles)	My dad says that white people run South Africa. Are you sure you're from South Africa?
(Afram)	I don't know. Maybe North Africa.
(Charles)	What language do they speak in Africa?
(Afram)	Swahili
(Charles)	Say something in Swahili.
(Afram)	I can't!
(Charles)	Why? Your parents tell you not to?
(Afram)	No, I just don't know any Swahili.

40 African-Americans

(Charles) Do you know any African songs?
(Afram) No.
(Charles) Jose says he's Mexican-American. He knows lots of Mexican songs.
(Afram) So what? Just because he can sing Mexican ain't no big deal. Did you know the Egyptians were black and they built the pyramids?
(Charles) Really! I didn't know that. When was that?
(Afram) I don't know. Two thousand years ago, I think.
(Charles) Why should you call yourself something different just because your great-great-grand parents came from Africa. My great grandfather came from Germany. I don't see anything different. Don't you like being an American?
(Afram) I am different! I'm black.
(Charles) My mom says that just because people have different colors, doesn't make them different. She says we're all Americans.
(Afram) You just don't know anything. I have to go home now.
 . . . .Mom, Why do I have to call myself an African-American?

Afram won't have positive feelings from this exchange.

Darker-skinned people have stress living in societies dominated by color conscious pale-skinned people. Having a strong positive self-image is one defense against the stress. Adopting false, unclear titles such as African-American increases confusion and stress. It becomes especially difficult for children to define themselves.

Cultural Influence

Calling oneself African-American is like saying there is a red rainbow in the sky. The term has no meaning. There can be no rainbow unless there is an arc of concentric bands of the colors of the spectrum. You can have the colors of red, blue, yellow, etc., without having a rainbow. But you can't have a rainbow without those colors. This is also true for the American culture. Countries can be of various African and European cultures and not be American. It cannot be American without having a mixture of these cultures. In saying this, I don't mean to imply that Asian nations have not also contributed to American culture.

Kidnaped Africans and their descendants have strongly influenced American culture. It doesn't matter that Africans spent their early years in this country as enslaved kidnaped victims. Their presence had as great an impact on American culture as did other groups.

America culture evolved from the interaction between Hausas, Mandingos, Yorubas, Sengalese, English, Germans, Chinese and others ethnic groups. These cultures exist in other parts of the world. There they are distinct cultures. But, it takes the cultural mixture of all of them to make it American culture.

I am not implying that the experiences of all Americans are the same. They aren't. The rich, middle class and the poor all have different experiences in America. Males and females have different experiences here, as do those with different skin colors. But it's the combination that makes it the American experience.

If Africans had not come, American history and culture would be different. Leaving them out of historical records doesn't remove their cultural influence from society. Like the unique flavor hickory chips add to the taste of barbecue, their presence added a unique flavor to American culture. This flavor is missing from the culture of European nations.

Since they were excluded from history, people tend to devalue African people's contributions to American culture. This is a mistake. Their contributions were just as valuable as those of the Europeans. The big difference is that the rewards for their contributions were stolen by others.

America benefitted and prospered from the labors of both. The pale-skinned workers received pay for their labors, but the enslaved kidnaped victim did not. This doesn't diminish their work in building this country. Without the African contribution, there is a good chance that the United States of America would not exist.

If America had lost the Revolutionary War, I doubt that the European nations would have allowed it to gain the strength to fight another one. Africans, freemen and slaves, played a direct role in the winning of that war.

During the early stages of the war, General George Washington didn't want men of African ancestry in the Continental Army. He had the Continental Congress pass a resolution barring them from service [7] Then he had problems getting colonial Europeans to volunteer. Congress even offered them land and money as inducements, but they still didn't join the army and navy in significant numbers. Finally, after the winter at Valley Forge when thousands of those who had enlisted had deserted the American army, Washington changed his mind. Desperate, he directed congress to change the law barring Africans from the army. He welcomed Africans in America's war of independence.

Africans, both enslaved and free, joined the fight for American independence. Haitians, the Fontages Legion, also came to help the colonists fight for independence.[8] It is very likely that the colonists would have lost the war if the Africans had not volunteered to fight. Americans of African ancestry have fought in all of America's wars.

Along with labor, Americans of African ancestry have contributed to scientific and industrial advancement. We have added culture with songs, books, poems, dance steps and grammatical expressions. Records of our pain, our defeats, our hopes and our accomplishments are all an integral part of America.

Label

Racial hatred and discrimination causes pain and suffering for oppressed groups. This causes many individuals to seek separation from what they call white-America. They do it by adopting hyphenated titles like African-American. Groups must use caution and reason before acting. Otherwise, they act in ways that harm their cause. People categorize themselves when they adopt the African-American label. American is the name for citizens of the USA. Groups that modify that name to identify themselves (African-American, Asian-American, or Mexican-American) are declaring themselves to be a modified version of genuine Americans. These people devalue their own claim to citizenship rights when they adopt these labels. With their own categorization, they are saying people with African ancestors or dark skin aren't real Americans.

This advances the cause of racists who always have claimed the United States as "white man's" country. They believe Africans, Mexicans, Chinese and others can work here and fight in the country's wars but they aren't real citizens. Before, they used derogatory ethnic slurs to separate these groups from "real" Americans. Now they don't have to, because these groups voluntarily separate and name themselves. Multiculturalism sweeps the country without resistance, because it serves their interests.

African-American, Asian-American, Mexican-American and others are labels of division. They cause resentment in those who previously were not bigots. Many people don't know how shamefully dark-skinned people were treated in America's past. Confused about the motives for using these labels, outsiders believe the group wants to isolate itself.

African-Americans might have an answer to these charges. These are some rebuttals they might make. Who cares what they think? They're the ones with the problem, because they act from ignorance. My heritage is important to me and I'm not going to let other people's attitude keep me from relating to it.

I would tell them that we are involved in a life and death struggle and not some petty social game. We must reason critically and act in positive ways if we are to survive. We could ignore opinion if the idea of African-Americanism both strengthened our resolve and attracted allies. Instead it weakens resolve by confusing the group's image. It makes enemies of neutral citizens. It shouldn't be used.

Wrap twin statues in different colored paper. Have people unwrap them and note their reactions. Most will comment that you have two identical statues. Few will comment on the different colored wrapping paper. Repeat the experiment only this time label each package differently. Most people will ask what the difference is between the statues. Although their eyes tell them they are identical, people are more inclined to believe the labeling that says they're different. Usually, people will accept identical items wrapped differently without much fuss. In almost all cases, identical items labeled differently will surprise and bother them.

The same is true with people. Some will expect you to be different, because you have a different skin color. When they see your desires and beliefs are similar to their own, your wrapping (skin color) is less important. Everybody expects you to be different when you label yourself as different. Bigots already label people differently according to skin color. Most people know about their hatred and ignore them. However when you label yourself African-American and different, people will treat you as different. You won't be pleased by the different way they treat you. Americans are suspicious and intolerant of groups who insist on being different. They make little effort to understand or get along with them. Historically they have not treated them well.

For many, the discovery of Africa as an ancestral home was empowering. Joyful knowledge of their ancestors as complete people, leaders and inhabitants of African nations, electrified their souls. Here was information confirming what they always had known in their hearts. Their ancestors had a grand existence long before they were kidnaped and enslaved. The `black' race was equal to other races. Americans with dark skin had a traceable

African-Americans 45

genetic path just as pale-skinned Americans did. Knowing this is more important than anything else they will ever learn.

Babies are excited when they discover their fingers, toes and other body parts. Learning to wiggle and control them is fun. The fun and games of playing with these parts help the child learn how to control them for future use. Playing with them serves a purpose, but that isn't the purpose for their existence.

For many, their African heritage is a newly discovered part of themselves. They need to explore it, play with it, and come to know it. But they must remember that it's only information. It's useful as a tool for self development, but useless as a worshipful idol. Use it to heal the soul- scarring wounds caused by centuries of exclusion and oppression. Don't use it as an identity for supermen or as an escape mechanism.

Sadly, people are using their African heritage as an escape mechanism, a magical path to the promised land. Calling themselves African-Americans or often just Africans, they adopt African dress. They replace American customs with African customs, or at least what someone told them were African customs. African styles are beautiful and grand additions to one's wardrobe. However, one indulges in fantasy when they believe ancient African customs and dress protect them from present oppression. One can be blinded from present realities when they become too fixated in the past.

People on the African continent have made impressive accomplishments. So have those on the Asian and European continents. This shows that people of all skin colors have had periods of greatness. Knowing this gives one the information they need to correct historical distortions showing Africans as only savages. But, we are not Africans. We can neither become Africans, nor return to our ancestors' times. Our challenge is learning to survive in modern America.

People don't develop and adopt cultural ways as momentary styles of living. Successful cultures develop customs and mores as life sustaining mechanisms. They are the tried and true ways of doing things that ensure group survival. Ritual and custom are ways of teaching the young how to survive. They also provide a group with emotional comfort and stability. Climate, geography, food availability and competing neighbors are factors that help mold people's culture. Skin color does not decide culture. Also, cultural ways change as survival needs change.

People living near large bodies of water usually depend on it to sustain their lives. Large fishing fleets usually play a big role in their survival. They also use the sea for traveling and trading. As a result, their culture and customs will evolve in directions that increase their knowledge and skills at extracting a living from the sea. Fishing, swimming, ship building, and celestial navigating are skills they will cultivate. Their prayers, songs and dances will be about the sea. These songs will teach the youth about sea life and about the nation's historical use of the sea.

Different customs and modes of dress will evolve in mountainous areas, tropical forest or flat inland areas. If they are farmers, they will pray for rain, insect control, and fertile soil. Their customs will help their children learn about weather patterns, soil use and conservation, plants and animals. Their tools of survival will be different from those of sailors.

If a sea-faring family moves inland, it would have to change customs. Reverence for deep sea fishing, ship building and celestial navigating skills must be replaced by farming customs. Teaching the children about their ancestors would still be important, but not as important as teaching them to survive in the new environment.

Americans are confused about the value of maintaining past cultural values. Pale-skinned Americans use cultural traditions from European nations as evidence proving their superiority to other groups. Dark-skinned Americans counter these with cultural traditions from African nations. Mexicans, Koreans, and other groups join in with their own cultural versions. It is not in the interest of the country to use cultural values this way. Used this way, it causes conflicts that damage national harmony.

People in European nations each needed certain cultural values and customs to survive there. Those from African and Asian

African-Americans 47

nations needed different ones to survive. All of them adopted new ones for surviving in America. We are descendants of those who adapted successfully.

Those who would be African-Americans are moving in the wrong direction. They teach their children the survival techniques of societies and environments that no longer exist. Even if successful they will not have improved their chances for survival in America. They and their children will be African experts in an American environment.

Picture a family from a seafaring nation that moves inland to a farming nation. Proud of his heritage, the father teaches his sons a lot about ships and the sea, and little about the land and farming. As adults, his sons will not have the skills necessary to be successful farmers. At best, they can expect a future as hired unskilled labor on another man's farm. The father has assured that his sons would know the ways of their ancestors. But he didn't prepare them to compete in their own world.

Children of African-Americans suffer the same fate. They lose competitiveness when they learn to value the culture of their ancestors over the values of America where they must live. People must educate themselves about surviving in the times and environment in which they live. Life doesn't give them a choice. Give up the romantic notion that one need only study in areas that pleases them. They must understand the cultural values, customs and business practices of the American economy. This training begins at a very early age and continues throughout life.

Children with dark skin already face the hurdles of discrimination when they compete in the American economy. If we teach them to compete by African rules, instead of American rules, we handicap them further. This is like teaching a child about sailboats when they must compete in motor boat races. The art of sailing is noble but of little use to the child in a motorboat race. On their own the child may learn to start and drive the motorboat. Still, they are far behind when they finally get started, and probably will race with less skill then those better trained.

Culture and History

I recognize the need people have for knowing their history. But getting this knowledge must not come before learning how to survive. Learning the skills needed for surviving comes before everything else.

Learning history is part of cultural indoctrination. This helps the young understand the reasons for observing certain customs. People are displaced from their history when they leave their ancestral homeland. Then history takes a different dimension. They learn the history where they live so they can learn survival skills needed there. They learn the history of their ancestor's homeland so that they can understand how they lived. This allows them to maintain some contact with their ancestors.

Immigrants and displaced people must understand the value that each history has for their children, and keep them in perspective. Also, people must ensure that they are learning true history. Be careful not to learn and repeat the contrived history made up by your oppressors. It is equally important not to teach a contrived history made up by well meaning leaders from your own group.

American history has been distorted for centuries. Much to the embarrassment of the ruling minority, these distortions are being revealed. The true nature of Christopher Columbus' mistreatment of indigenous Americans is an example of this. Revelations about his torture and enslavement of the native Americans make a lie of him as a heroic Christian explorer. Other historical documents about the founding fathers of the country show that they were not as noble and religious as the history books have pictured them.

When the history of European nations is studied closely, one finds periods when many of its pale-skinned peasants were legally enslaved. There were also instances of child abuse and abandonment on a massive scale. As we learn more of this history we will know that the idea of European cultural or moral superiority is myth. People who have based their self-esteem on these myths are in trouble. They will suffer image confusion and self-esteem problems. Citizens of European nations have made some notable contributions in science and the arts. For financial gain, they also have forced barbaric and inhumane economic systems on their own citizens and others.

Americans of African ancestry will learn the same lessons as did their pale-skinned American brothers. Ancestors were imperfect people whose acts make weak foundations for building ones self-esteem.

The ancestors of both groups were successful in the most important way. They were strong and resourceful enough so that they lived to pass on their genes. Whether these genes pass to future generations depends on our abilities to survive modern day challenges. One cannot rely solely on the fact that one has pale or dark skin to survive.

When one insists on being recognized as different because of their African ancestry, they enter the racist game. Even worse, they play by the rules of bigots. They are acknowledging behavioral differences based on race and are now trying to show that the dark-skinned not the pale-skinned race is superior. You can read the most elementary books on genetics to know that skin color has no relation to intelligence. Even easier, you only need look at American society.

The genetic differences between a chimpanzee and a human are apparent. The dullest human is far superior in intellect to the smartest chimpanzee. Even brain damaged humans are superior to the smartest chimpanzee. No chimpanzee has ever exceeded the intelligence of a normal human. You can use this information to make claims for genetic superiority. From the physical identification alone, you can always conclude that this animal is intellectually inferior to any human.

Skin color does not give you enough information to decide intellectual superiority. You cannot accurately say that a pale-skinned American will always be intellectually superior to a darker-skinned one. If there is just one dark-skinned individual that is smarter than one pale-skinned individual, then group labels of genetic superiority must be discarded. Statistics showing intelligence difference between artificially grouped people are valueless. In the United States of America there are millions of dark-skinned individuals who are intellectually superior to hundreds of millions of pale-skinned persons. The reverse is also true. This proves that the intellect of a person cannot be determined by skin color. End of argument. They may prove something about the comparative ways people are treated in American society, but they do not prove intellectual superiority.

It makes no sense for a group of people to base their self-esteem on a factor such as skin color. Dark-skinned people must fight oppression based on skin coloring. It is a big mistake to fight this oppression by adopting a label that is based on skin color. When you do so you help racist bigots. As long as Americans label people ethnically, people within those groups will decide human values based on those labels.

You open yourself to group stereotyping and valuation when you claim a different name because of skin color (African-American). Racists have always claimed that dark-skinned people were different and of less value as citizens. It's a mistake to accept the artificial label of African-American that is already loaded with centuries of negative racist stereotyping. The arguments of both groups are factually unsupported. It is senseless to engage in verbal battles claiming superiority based on skin color.

"African-Americans" use the following European argument to justify their label.

"If people from Europe can call themselves Europeans, people from Africa can call themselves Africans. Both terms identify people by continents and not nations."

This is correct if one means only to describe a general area of the world where people live. Other than that it has no meaning.

Being an American is different from being an African, Asian or European. Although the USA is not the only nation on the American continents, its citizens are the only people who call themselves Americans. When one says American, they speak of people with one free democratic government, in a capitalistic

African-Americans

economic system, sharing a common language, and having religious freedom. They also speak of an American spirit and culture. This isn't true elsewhere. There is no universal European type of government, economic system, or language. None exists on the African and Asian continents either. There are more than thirty European countries speaking sixty major languages. There are more than fifty African countries speaking in excess of fifty major languages and thousands of dialects.[9] Swedes, Italians, Frenchmen and Russians live in Europe but have vastly different customs and governments. Which group, if any, is the typical European? Ethiopians, Ghanaians and Zulus live in Africa. Since all are different in government, language and culture, which group represents the typical African?

Americans, especially those less educated, tend to blur these distinctions. They relate to the separate countries on these continents as they do the individual American states. With indoctrination, they easily accept the false notion of a universal African, Asian or European culture. They also believe that people from each of these continents have a universal way of thinking. A history of continual wars between European nations, African nations and Asian nations reveals the falsity of such beliefs.

People from each of these continents have some similarities in skin colors and hair textures. Racists use these similarities as a way of applying stereotypical African, Asian and European traits to people. Then they claim that skin color indictates what people's culture and intelligence will be. By using skin color as a code for culture and intelligence, they totally exclude environment. Other people fall into this bigoted way of thinking when they use the names of continents to label their culture.

Ironically, when people assume the African-American identity, they are forcing themselves into the racist trap, not escaping from it. A standard African behavior doesn't exist. Writers from Europe created the stereotyped images of a standard African.

Black-Americans

What should we call ourselves if not African-American? Are we `black' Americans? No! That's no more descriptive than African-American. People use the term "blacks" to refer to American citizens with recognizable African ancestry. I say recognizably African, because millions of pale-skinned Americans also have African ancestors. Since we aren't black, using black as a descriptive label isn't accurate.

Labels of `black'-American and `black's are obviously wrong. I have never personally seen a person with black skin coloring. Even people with dark brown skin coloring are distinctive from their black hair. There may be groups of people with black skin. It would be as attractive as any other. However, truly black skin is less common than skin with shades of brown.

What are people saying when they identify themselves as black? People with chocolate, tea, or vanilla colored skin cannot all be `black` people. Even if they are descendant from people with black skin, that description no longer fits them. One rarely, if ever, sees truly black or truly white human skin. But America's media, government institutions and private industry divide people into `black' and `white' categories.

What self-images do `black' people hold? What images do others carry of them? Who is the government talking about when they give health, crime and census figures about `black' people? If not skin color, what standards are used to decide who `black' people are? There must be standards for the definitions to have meaning.

Black is used to show race. It means black skinned people who live or whose ancestors lived on the African continent. This definition is vague. People on the African continent have different cultures and physical appearances. Somalians, Zulus and Pygmies have wide differences. There are also differences between people of Africa's west coast. African ancestors of most Americans were kidnaped from this area. Ashantis, Dahomeans, Ibos, Mandingos,

African-Americans 53

Yorubas and others from this area have varying cultures and appearances.[10] Black doesn't accurately describe them nor their American descendants who are a greater mixture of people. The term `black' or `black'-American describes `white' people not `black' people. It doesn't describe people who are black; it describes people who aren't "white." Nobody really cares what a `black' person really is, just so it's clear what they are not. We can describe things by what they include or exclude. Kosher food describes by exclusion. Kosher food excludes pork, horse meat, shellfish and parts of cows and lambs. Degree of contamination doesn't count. For Jews, food is either Kosher or non Kosher. Americans use the same idea when they label people as `black' or "white."

`White' people describe all Americans in reference to themselves. People are either `white' or "nonwhite" (`black'). No matter how pale their skin is, Americans with African ancestors cannot be `white'. `White' people don't care about differences in skin color, culture, or other physical characteristics between African people. They don't care how distant the African ancestors may be. A person has them or they don't. A person is either `black' or "white." There are no degrees.

So being `black' in America definitely says what you aren't. It tells you nothing about what the person is. The idea of passing as `white' proves the point. Passing refers to people with straight hair, pale skin and an African ancestor. They have a physical appearance that makes them look `white'; they have an ancestor that makes them nonwhite. According to American racists' thinking, they are `black' passing for "white." It's not important to look for qualities that really make a person `black'. Nobody cares. America looks only for qualities making them nonwhite.

> Race - Beginning in 1976, the Federal government's data systems classified individuals into the following racial groups: American Indian or Alaskan Native, Asian or Pacific Islander, black, and white . . . Before 1989, if the

parents were of different races and one was white, the child was assigned the other parent's race. . . .
(p322 Health United States and Prevention Profile 1991)

It's clear that Americans have no sound reasons for calling themselves "Blacks." There are good reasons for not doing so. Calling people `black' is like calling them trash. Trash is a collection of undefined things that have little value. You only announce that you haven't met the standards for being "white." Do you want to identify yourself as something that isn't? Would Americans living in Texas accept being called non-Californians? If the Dodgers defined all baseball players as Dodgers or Ballers. Do you think all the other professional players would describe themselves as Ballers?

Being `white' also is a mythical condition and not descriptive of a race. People aren't white and don't have white skin. They have pale skin with ruddy or olive tones. There are no set standards for being `white.'

Americans constantly change qualifications for inclusion into this mythical group. In 1989 the governments National Vital Statistics System started designating a child's race by the race of the mother. A woman designated as `white' will only have `white' children after 1989. However, if she were married to a nonwhite man, all their children before 1989 would be nonwhite. The race of siblings born to the same parents a year apart will be different.

Before 1950, Americans also had yellow and red people. Chinese and Japanese were in the yellow race. `White-Americans' used these labels for stereotyping. They dropped the term when the Japanese objected to its use and when it no longer served a purpose. The idea of a yellow race has been so completely erased that few people born after 1945 know it existed. The idea of Native Americans as Redskins also has died. If it were not for old western movies and the crude naming of sports teams, this idea also would be completely extinct. Yellow and red-skinned people never existed. Like black, these were ways of showing a condition of being nonwhite.

African-Americans

`White' people cannot exist without `black' people. Mythical yellow and red people are gone. Being `white' is meaningless if mythical `black' people disappear. This frightens pale-skinned people whose self-image and self-esteem are totally based on the idea of whiteness.

Having pale skin and being `white' is not the same. There are many pale-skinned people who aren't "white." These pale-skinned people rely on a sense of self and individual accomplishments for identity. Their self-image wouldn't change if, like the yellow race, the idea of `black' and `white' races disappeared with the evening sun.

Ruling elites use whiteness to hide what are really class differences. The idea of whiteness influenced poor southerners to fight the rich man's civil war. They had slave labor, so rich plantation owners had a big advantage over poor people and small farmers. Yet these poor people fought for the rich man's right to keep slaves and his advantage over them. They did so as rich plantation owners' sons avoided the fighting. Poor people weren't fighting for states' rights issues, because most lacked the education needed to understand them. Blinded to their own exploitation, they fought for the cause of whiteness.

After the war, rich men legalized a two-tier pay system. `White' men were paid at a higher rate than `black' men. `White' men again praised this advantage for whiteness. They changed their minds when they realized that the rich men were bypassing them to hire the lower paid `black' worker. Whiteness caused them to attack the darker-skinned workers instead of the rich man's system that exploited them. In various forms, rich men have continued exploiting `white' taxpayers and workers. They are successful, because Americans are distracted by the idea of whiteness. First they use whiteness to cover their exploitative policies. When their schemes are uncovered, they flag `white' rage onto their `black' scapegoats. We must discard blackness. Then maybe we can save our pale-skinned brothers and ourselves from the plague of whiteness.

African-Americans

Americans aren't blacks, whites, Africans, Asians, or Europeans. We're an entirely new breed of people. We created and are the creation of this nation. We are a mixture of European, Native American and African people. If we still practice African customs, they are modified by exposure to American pressures.

Even if we are African with no European, Asian or Native American genes, we are still an American mixture of African genes. Those genes have survived in an American environment. Physically, emotionally, and culturally we are a new people. Our ancestors were transplanted. We are the new American people (AmPers).

We are AmPers with dark brown, brown, light brown, tan and pale skin. Americans with European ancestors also are AmPers. They aren't English, German, Polish or Italian. Even if they have only European ancestors, they are a mixture of many European people. Many practice their ancestors' customs, but they do so with American influence. Even the language is different. English is spoken as a native tongue in America and England. Although we can understand each other, English is culturally different in each country.

Two hundred years have passed and still America's pale-skinned leaders nurse at the breast of Europe. They insist on calling ours a western culture. They insist that it is European. Economically and militarily America is the leader of the world, but still they maintain the myth of Europe as the center of the world. They are like middle aged males fearfully relying on their frail old fathers, who long ago lost their vitality.

Change will come in spite of them. America is a new force in the world separate from Europe and its nations. Youth will set uniquely American standards with or without the old guard's participation. Americans have more in common with each other, than they have with people of similar skin colors on other continents.

The American experience makes people Ampers. Some suffer oppression because of their skin color, sex or ethnic group.

African-Americans

Others enjoy prosperity. It is the interaction of all these experiences that makes American culture.

We need to eliminate oppression from our culture. We do so by embracing our Americanism not denying it. The idea of AmPer is the only way that oppression and national discord will be eliminated. Taking the real identity of American person (AmPers) has advantages. It's a real identity. It's an identity of inclusion. People include themselves, because they want to be identified as the new American. Secondly, it forces the opposition, not you, to adopt labels of opposition.

People living on the American continents have the potential for being the modern Egyptians and Greeks. They can forge their mixture of people into advanced new cultures. They can be Mexicans, Canadians, or American Persons (AmPers). Or they can remain African, Asia and European descendants.

Opposing arguments could say that the reality of life in American society is that people are separated by skin color and race. People are labeled and oppressed under those labels. In resisting, they must use the same labeling. This identifies the group, giving it cohesion and strength. They would argue that an idea of AmPers must wait for better times.

I agree that oppression against racial groups is real in America. But the idea of AmPers must exist before the problem can be solved. People can form resistive groups, but they must do so within Americanism. They can think of themselves as `blacks' and `whites' with separate cultures living in separate communities. Or they can think of themselves as American people with varying skin colors, some of whom are being oppressed.

Within the first view, each mythical community is responsible for its own problems. This is convenient for the stronger and richer `white' group. They can absolve themselves of any responsibility for conditions in the `black' community. If they do decide to help, they do so with a sense of charity, not responsibility.

`Black' leaders also find this view convenient. It isolates and groups darker-skinned citizens apart from other Americans, thus creating a separate community. Agreeing that the mythical `black' community is responsible for its own problems creates a `black' leaders' role. Most `black' people will suffer from this arrangement. By dividing token government funds among themselves, `black' leaders will live as luxuriously as their `white' counterparts.

Taking the view that we are one American community with various skin colors creates different possibilities. People can consider themselves Americans and still recognize that they suffer oppression .

There is a difference between the idea of a pale-skinned group of Americans oppressing dark-skinned Americans and the idea of whites oppressing blacks (African-Americans). In the first situation, people still see themselves as one nation even though they evaluate each other by skin color. Internal inequalities don't prevent them from forming a common bond against foreigners. In the second situation, people feel they are separate groups sharing the same country. They believe that they have separate cultures and interests. Often, groups feel closer to foreigners who have a similar skin color than they do to other groups here. This causes pale skinned Americans to side with European people against fellow dark-skinned Americans. Also, dark-skinned people and those of Asian descent would have the same loyalty for Africans and Asians respectively. Hyphenated labels (African-American, Italian American, Chinese-American, etc.) tend to encourage these feelings.

We have a better chance of resolving the problems caused by attitudes in the first situation than we do the second. When people see themselves as one American community, they are more likely to question unfair practices against other members. It becomes harder to keep them separate based on insignificant differences such as skin color. They'll be more diligent in searching out real causes for economic inequalities.

For example, let's examine the problem of income distribution in America. As a group, dark-skinned Americans have less income than others. When compared to pale-skinned

African-Americans 59

Americans, a higher percentage of them live in poverty. We could take the "black vs white" community attitude and look for the problem only in the mythical `black' community. We'll find many causes there, but never the true one. Or we could examine all of American society for answers to the problem.

Usually, people's lifetime incomes are affected by the quality of their education. Statistics show that high school graduates make much more money over their lifetime than high school dropouts do. There are even wider differences in income between high school and college graduates.

For most of its existence, American society has restricted dark-skinned Americans to inferior schooling. Some students were still attending these inferior segregated schools in the seventies. Federal, state and local government policies continued this practice. In view of the proven connection between schooling and income, it is clear that governmental policy guaranteed low income for many dark-skinned Americans.

Less then twenty-five years ago dark-skinned Americans were still fighting segregated school systems. In the Mississippi case, *Alexander v. Holmes,* the U.S. Supreme court ruled that school segregation must end at once. This decision came in October 1969. In 1971 the court was still ruling against school districts that were segregating. This book is being written in 1993, so less than twenty-two years have passed since this particular ruling was made. This ruling didn't make equal schooling available to all dark-skinned Americans.

Under perfect conditions, twenty-two years is not enough time to undo centuries of poverty caused by government policies. Children entering the system in 1971 would just be graduating from college. As of yet they would have no impact on the community.

These facts show that external forces are directly responsible for much of the poverty suffered by dark-skinned Americans. `Black' people in `black' communities didn't cause these conditions. Why are they alone expected to correct them? The American government of all the people caused these problems by marking dark-skinned citizens for discrimination. Governments at

60 African-Americans

every level and all citizens have a responsibility for correcting the situation.
    Those targeted for oppression must fight hardest against it. Leaders will spring up to inspire them. These leaders form action groups and label them. Sometimes they create the impression of false relations where none exist. People shouldn't let these leaders think for them. The need for joining in group resistance doesn't prove the existence of a particular culture. People can have a strong sense of comradeship and dedication to cause and not be fused in other areas of their lives.
    Many oppressed people make a common error in thinking. On the one hand they resist stereotyping because of skin color. On the other they claim a culture based on it. Those calling themselves African-Americans are making this error. Based mainly on skin color, they claim certain African cultural and behavioral traits. However, they are resentful when others use this same skin color to make cultural and behavioral assumptions of their own. Americans cannot allow themselves to engage in faulty thinking like this.
    People cannot rationally analyze social problems when the cling to false ideas of racial community. The practice of thinking racially has existed for so long in America that it will be hard to change. Many people need to change beliefs about group stereotypes. Then they must reevaluate their relationship with the group.
    We must have precise meanings of words and expressions before we use them. Otherwise, we will not have a clear understanding of situations we think or talk about. Here are some questions that will help you clarify your understanding about certain terms.

I.   A. Exactly what do you mean when you say, this is a black person?
        1. Are you giving a physical description, a cultural description or what?

2. What is your definition or description of a black person?
3. What mental picture or feeling do you have when you use this term?
4. Using your definition, what important information do you communicate to others when you say someone is black?

B. Does answering the questions in section "A" increase your understanding of how you and others use this term?

C. With your new understanding, can you say that this term accurately describes you? Does it accurately describe all the others so named?

D. Should you be more selective in using this term? Should you stop using it?

E. Substitute "white people" in place of "black people" in section A. Now answer it again. Do the same for African-American, Mexican-American, Latino, Chicano, etc.

II. 1. What is your definition for culture?
2. Exactly what is your definition of African, Asian, Latino and European culture?
3. Should you be using these terms if you don't have a precise definition for them?
4. Do you believe that people can remain culturally separate after living together for four hundred years?

USARIAN...I AM

Continents of Heritage
Africa Just One
Varied Such Bloodlines
Of Cultures They've Come

This Land Conceived
Miscegenation has Bred
A Modern Genealogy
Apprehensive the Tread

A New Race of Mankind
Only Yesterday Born
Historically No Lineage
That Strength To Lean On

Once They were Negroes
Then Black They Became
Decades of Frustration
In Search of a Name

America By Birthright
This USA, Their Land
A Soul of That Soil
USArian.....I am

James B Earley

Reprinted Courtesy USARIAN ARTS, BOX 4043, Vallejo, CA 94590

IMAGE

"WE MUST RECOGNIZE AND COUNTER THE FORCES AIMED AT DESTROYING OUR SELF-ESTEEM."

Oppressed citizens include women and people of African, Asian, and Hispanic ancestry. Collectively they make up the majority of United States citizens. Still, they all face discrimination from a powerful minority group. What is the secret of this powerful minority? Control over the minds of the majority. This control is so effective and complete that the thoughts of most of the citizens are manipulated without their knowing it. Even worse, in their ignorance they often help to spread negative stereotypes about themselves.

Oppressed people must gain control of their thoughts and emotions. A person's thoughts and beliefs can either empower or limit them. Self-doubt and low self-esteem destroy the will to succeed. Talents are useless when others control how you see yourself. If your sex or skin color makes you feel inferior, it is your own thinking that defeats you. Others aren't naturally superior; you've made yourself inferior with your own thoughts. The results are the same. They win more of the good things in life. Negative thinking and low self-esteem always reduce your opportunities for success.

Realizing that you engage in negative thinking is an important first step toward change. But, just knowing it is not enough. You must have a plan to change negative thinking patterns. Since negative propaganda is continuous, your defenses against it must be continuous.

Writers and speakers criticize American citizens of African ancestry for their low self-esteem. However, most of them fail to show workable ways for change. They increase feelings of insecurity by continually highlighting group faults without accompanying corrective solutions. American citizens of African ancestry face this experience daily.

The media assumes they are a group of like individuals. Then it uses the crimes and failings of the few to stereotype all group members. You are inescapably caught in a trap of low self-esteem if you believe their faulty logic. In their logic you will always be a skin color and never an individual.

Many Americans from oppressed groups have pushed through the barriers of sexism and racism. In doing so, they gain more control over their lives and futures. These active people know what others must still learn. Struggles for power and dignity never end. One must learn and continuously use effective tactics to obtain and protect their rights. If they don't, they will always suffer from oppression.

Ruling elites do not give up power voluntarily. They have small concern for individuals from weak unorganized groups. Those who seek power must understand its character and nature. Self-discipline, determination and a positive self-image are character traits of winners. People with strong positive self-images are the only ones who escape mental manipulation. A strong self-esteem guards them from weak destructive attitudes. Rulers have these traits. They work at destroying them in those they choose to oppress.

A powerful ruling male minority uses divisive tactics to control the majority. They have divided United States' society into groups. Dividing people into sexual, racial and ethnic groups is the usual tactic. Image makers attach certain traits and characteristics to group members.

Society treats people from different groups in different ways. Group association often decides what image people have of themselves. Positive group images can bring opportunities and rewards that exceed those warranted by a person's talents. The opposite, a negative image, can bring prejudice, discrimination and lost opportunities.

Waves of propaganda reinforce false group images. Misrepresenting group images, it misleads people to think of group members in biased ways. Media (newspapers, books, movies and television) create and perpetuate group stereotypes.

These propaganda campaigns are so effective that people in the targeted groups frequently adopt these biased images of themselves. They believe they are less intelligent and less attractive than the power group. Negative thinking becomes an internalized force driving them to greater depths of self hate, hopelessness and despair.

These people see themselves as inadequate to handle their own affairs and unworthy of exercising political power. They believe the myth that pale-skinned males are superior and ideally suited for rule. Being ruled by anyone else, even someone like themselves, seems unnatural. Defeated, they accept the power group's right to use oppressive practices. Evil practices that rob groups of their citizenship rights are accepted as normal. They work harder for special favors than at finding ways to end their oppression.

We often get laws passed against specific acts of oppression. Many of these laws are poorly written because they don't address the real causes of the problem. Sometimes they create special treatment for one oppressed group. Many of them eventually are reversed. Some are just ignored by the power group.

Campaigns to eliminate oppression often do not work because they try to carry people where they feel unworthy of going. These leaders don't understand how badly their troops have been wounded by the psychological propaganda wars. Weak and confused, many wounded wish to be carried, not led.

A right attitude is needed for anyone who expects to win a contest. This is especially true for those fighting oppression. The consequences for losing are serious. Poverty, loss of freedom, poor health care and even death awaits oppressed people who lose. Powerful elites will use cruel and deadly force to retain their advantages. Oppressed groups must be as equally determined. They must seize control of their thinking processes. If they don't, the powerful minority's propaganda campaign will continue to be effective.

Females show the effectiveness of mind control. More than half the population, they hold less than 5 percent of the political offices. They continue to vote males into office although men historically pass laws hostile to female interests. As a voting majority, women should have changed sexist laws decades ago. Americans of African ancestry also have failed to act in their own interests. Though in the minority as voters, we still have the means to improve our social and economic situation.

There are key actions that members of oppressed groups must take. First, they must learn to recognize the psychological weapons that turn them against themselves. Next, they must remove the power of these weapons by changing their thinking. Then they need to engage in the continual process of repairing their damaged psyches.

Rights As Citizens

The false idea that pale-skinned males are the only natural leaders of the world must be changed. We also must destroy the idea that they have the responsibility and right to decide the extent to which others can exercise their rights.

Oppressed Groups have allowed a small group of pale-skinned males to:

1. set the qualifications that members of oppressed groups must meet to enjoy American citizenship rights.
2. set the time table they will follow in returning the stolen rights and privileges to members of Oppressed Groups.
3. limit the number of the stolen rights they will return to members of oppressed groups.

We must change our attitudes that allow this situation to continue.

The constitution of United States of America details how we become citizens. It outlines citizens' rights. All citizens have the same rights under the constitution. These rights are permanent.

Read the constitution and know your rights. Become fully conscious of them. Feel ownership of them in your heart. Feel anger over any that were stolen from you. Band with others to get them back. Face your oppressors as owners demanding a return of stolen property and not as an outsider begging for favors.

Amendment XIV
(Adopted to the constitution 1868)

Section 1 All **persons born or naturalized** in the United States, and subject to the jurisdiction thereof, are citizens of the United States and of the State wherein they reside. No State shall make or enforce any law which shall abridge the privileges or immunities of citizens of the United States; nor shall any State deprive any person of life, liberty, or property, without due process of law; nor deny to any person within its jurisdiction the equal protection of the laws.

This means that people are citizens because they were born here. Immigrants are citizens because they were naturalized. The origin of your ancestors has nothing to do with your citizenship rights. It doesn't matter where your parents or grandparents were born. If you were born in any part of the United States, you are a citizen. If you weren't born here but have been naturalized, you are a citizen. Naturalized citizens cannot become president.

The constitution doesn't give pale-skinned men greater rights. The date your ancestors came to America has no bearing on your rights as a citizen. People are committing criminal acts when they bar you from your rights. You commit a stupid act if you allow anyone to steal your rights without protest.

Power To Make Change

American society discriminates against brown-skinned Americans (Americans of African ancestry) and American females more then it does against any other group. It also targets the Hispanic, Asian and indigenous American for discrimination. Before, these conditions had to be tolerated because oppressed groups lacked economic and political power. This is no longer true. Most of the barriers to voting were eliminated during the sixties and seventies. Combined, oppressed groups are an overwhelming majority. Why do they allow the oppression to continue? The answer is simple. They have such a distorted self-image that they do not feel the equal of their oppressors.

Too many members of the Oppressed Groups doubt their ability to function as full citizens. Streams of propaganda have convinced them that they are inferior. Some have enough self-esteem to realize that the stereotypes do not apply to them as individuals. But, failing to carry their reasoning further, they still believe them true about others in their group. Some advance their thinking and reject all the stereotypes about their group. But they still believe the stereotypes about other oppressed groups.

Many Americans of African descent tend to believe stereotypes about Spanish speaking Americans. Persons with Spanish heritage, or those from countries on the Asian continent tend to believe stereotypes about dark-skinned American citizens. Males from all groups believe the ones about women. Pale-skinned women believe the stereotypes about other groups.

People have less concern when oppressed people look different or have different cultural traits. This is a mistake in logic. People should fight the oppression of weaker groups. By protecting weaker groups from oppression, citizens eliminate any future threat to their own rights. Even the strong lose when they let another group get oppressive powers. Although a particular oppressive law may not be directed at them, its passage takes rights from them and gives it to the power group. This is true because laws can be applied to all people, even though they are directed at one group.

One good example of this was the poll test law. Legislatures passed a law giving themselves the right to set voter standards. They refused to register anyone who failed their test. Pale-skinned citizens approved the law as a means to curb voting rights of citizens of African ancestry. This was very foolish. They restricted their own freedoms also.

The law gave powerful elites control over everyone's precious voting rights. Although they used their powers less frequently against pale-skinned citizens, they did so whenever it served their interests. Before the law was passed, everyone voted without restriction. After enacting the law, a small group controlled everyone's access to voting. Repealing it restored unrestricted voting rights to everybody.

Laws passed to fight illegal drug trade also weaken our constitutional protection. When we passed "No knock" and "asset confiscation" laws, we destroyed our own protection along with the drug dealers. It's now legal for the police to confiscate assets based on suspicion of drug activity. They keep the assets even if they never bring charges against the owner. The owner must prove his right to have his funds restored. This violates constitutional protection of due process. Many innocent people have lost money to the police because of this law. Predictably, the police confiscate more property from members in oppressed groups. But, all groups suffer since this law gives police the license to steal.

Groups that believe they're better than other oppressed groups won't cooperate with them. They're more likely to align themselves with the powerful male minority. These misguided people increase the strength of the dominant male minority group. This extends the era of oppression for everybody.

It's ironic that oppressed groups see the power group as an ally instead of as a common opponent. Each, at times, joins the dominant male minority in oppressing one or more of the other groups. They see this as a way of escaping the pit of oppression. These groups are splitting their forces and weakening their ability to end oppression.

The power group favors certain oppressed groups or individuals. They may give them special recognition or privilege. Koreans are praised as frugal. Chinese may be praised as studious. Asians are recognized as pseudo `white' people. These groups join in the oppression of the darker-skinned or Hispanic groups to show appreciation. This is short sighted. Special recognition does not protect people from discriminatory practices. People aren't free if their rights and privileges depend on others' charity.

The act of accepting special favors from the power group legitimizes their power to restrict and control your rights. People must own and control the things they give as gifts. This means that you and your oppressors must believe that they have legitimate power to control your rights. Otherwise they couldn't give them back to you as a special favor. So, the receivers of special favors are still dominated by the power group. People can only guarantee their rights by destroying the elite group's power to oppress.

Politicians refer to "black," Asian, Spanish and female votes during election campaigns. Referring to pockets of votes creates the false impression that each has different interests. Sadly, oppressed groups fall for this contrived thinking. They don't see that laws favoring one group threaten the freedom of all groups.

They solicit special laws favorable for their group. This alarms other groups. Soon each group fights for their own special interest laws. Competitive environments in equal rights legislation increases the ruling minority's power. Having these laws passed is dangerous for another reason. They imply that other people need special laws to get rights that pale-skinned males already have. This is wrong thinking. It falsely reinforces the idea that a small group of pale-skinned male rulers have more constitution rights and powers than others. We should work to destroy this false idea and not seek to give unconstitutional powers to other groups.

Instead, oppressed people attack each other for insignificant gains. Negative thinking keeps them on the merry-go-round of manipulation. This will continue until they abandon separatist thinking. Eventually they will understand that no group can win its freedom as long as it ignores the oppression of others.

People from different groups must cooperate to end oppression though they doubt the intelligence, morality or worthiness of others. They do not have to like each other. Mutual respect makes cooperative efforts easier, but it is not an absolute requirement. All must crave freedom and believe in the constitution. Rulers weaken everybody's constitutional protection, when they pass laws that eliminate any group's rights. There is only one constitution. The oppression of any group of American citizens should alarm all others.

Bigots believing in racial superiority should fight hardest for equal opportunity. They should demand distribution of rewards based on talent and performance. In such a society, their superiority would guarantee them the best of everything. This would be a perfect way for them to prove racial superiority.

This doesn't happen because they know they aren't superior. That's why they pass discriminatory laws and engage in discriminatory practices. These barriers give them the advantage over others who may be better qualified. If the rest of us are too dumb to stop them, maybe they deserve all the rewards.

Oppressed people often have problems finding an enemy to fight. The individual pale-skinned male is not an evil devil. Most of them are decent individuals. Although they don't know it, most of them also are victims of the policies of the powerful minority. Like the obviously oppressed, they are concerned with personal and family interests. The major difference is that most of them identify with the powerful minority.

Pale-skinned men are average humans. See them as no better nor worse then individuals from other groups. It has been a mistake to wrap them in cloaks of wisdom and strength; it would be a greater mistake to make them monsters. Some are evil. Some have been guilty of unspeakable crimes against Americans of African ancestry, native Americans and others. They have also oppressed their own mothers and daughters. But, so have males from other races.

Oppressed Groups must attack the power base of the dominant male group. Special privilege is the evil giving them oppressive powers. It would be a mistake to create a campaign of hate against pale-skinned males. We gain nothing by substituting one set of stereotypes for another.

Americans of African ancestry.

The predicament of American citizens of African ancestry, historically bad, is getting worse. If we accept the statistics, this group tops the lists of everything that is bad. They are at the bottom of lists suggesting the good things in life. Books give various reasons for this group's plight. The mental capacity of the `black' race is always questioned. Discrimination, the deficient educational system, and cultural differences all take their places as reasons for this condition.

Facts about this group are twisted and distorted. However, they accurately show a group suffering discrimination because of skin color. Discrimination creates formidable barriers to economic advancement and forces many of them into poverty. A poor self-image and low self-esteem adds to their problems.

Africans came to America both as free men and as chained kidnaped victims. They showed bravery, emotional stability and a powerful will to survive in the face of overwhelming odds. Private industry, government officials and church leaders all conspired to crush their spirit. These forces worked to destroy their dignity and self-esteem. Most resisted these attempts. Legal and economic injustice dogged them even after they gained freedom. A strong and courageous people, they persistently fought the injustice of denied rights.

Wars cause casualties. Wars of oppression cause debilitating emotional and mental wounds. Some become confused and are unable to evaluate their own actions. They have no personal standards of conduct by which to measure themselves. They become the school drop outs, drug addicts, alcoholics and criminals. Most pitiful are those functioning far below their potential, victimized by their own twisted thinking. They're lifelong victims.

Destructive Thoughts

From the time we are old enough to talk we're deluged with negative propaganda about our skin color. Much of it is delivered with such cunning that it enters our thinking without our knowing it. We lose the battle for control of our thinking without realizing we were at war.

In ways this war is like those we have with ants. When ants invade our home, we attack them with a poisoned spray. This kills some, but not all of them. The survivors continually return. We must destroy their nest to stop them. Finding the nest is normally impossible, so we let the ants carry the poison for us. We get some to take the bait. Blind to the danger they take it back to the nest. Ants pass the poisoned food to others and become destroyers of their own community.

Sadly, too many of us act like ants. We aid in the destruction of our self-images by carrying and repeating negative racial stereotypes. American citizens of African ancestry repeat them in their jokes and their daily conversations. They even repeat the negative stereotypes in their movies. Derogatory comments about the physical appearance of dark-skinned Americans of African ancestry have become standard. They refer to dark skin, thick lips, wide noses, kinky hair as ugly physical traits. Attributing these features to people, in anger or jest, is a put down.

Many claim its only fun. It isn't. It's an unrecognized source reenforcing negative stereotypes. Repeating insults that attack your image is sick humor, at best. Mentally and verbally you tell yourself that the image you see in the mirror every day is ugly. Your defenses are down when being entertained. That's why people listen to negative stereotypes about themselves in jokes or movies that they normally would not tolerate. Jokes are an easy and sneaky way to spread negative stereotypes about people.

During these periods the message enters the brain with no screening. The message of the joke becomes more acceptable with repetition. Soon, adults who used them in jest, come to believe them as fact. Negative messages have an especially devastating effect on children.

Parental talk creates the child's world. Learning from adults, they repeat and believe the negative stereotypes. When they hear their own parents saying that dark-skinned people are unattractive, immoral and lacking in skills, they believe it. They have no other choice.

From the cradle to the grave, American citizens of African ancestry hear negative comparisons of themselves. Frequently they hear them from people who look just like them. In comparison, they may hear that pale-skinned people are evil, but they also hear these people are strong, intelligent and attractive.

They also demean themselves in other ways. Remarks belittling the intelligence of `black' people, their work habits and business abilities are also common. Some individuals know the stereotypes are false, but repeat them for their comic value. Over time, negative stereotypes become the image other people accept about darker-skinned Americans and they about themselves.

Strong willed people can withstand verbal attacks from outsiders. Their defenses are weaker against attacks from family or group members. They have little defense against their own thoughts.

That's why thinking belittling thoughts about yourself is so destructive. Members of the group hear negative comments about themselves. This creates negative thoughts. They hear strong positive comments about pale-skinned people. This generates positive thoughts about them. The comparison leaves dark-skinned people feeling inferior. The more people think and express negative thoughts about themselves, the more unworthy they feel.

This destroys their self-esteem. Their positive accomplishments decline with a loss of self-esteem. The cycle continues. Declining positive accomplishments make the stereotypes more believable and drives self-esteem lower. What was previously only stereotyping, now becomes real character traits for many in the group.

Stereotypes become more believable with repetition. The stereotype about Black Americans not having the intelligence to run a business is such a stereotype. Another is that black tradesmen are unreliable and do sloppy work. Americans of African descent repeat these stereotypes. Some common ones are as follows. `Black' businesspeople cheat you. `Black' owned stores have higher prices and poor products. `Black' people do poor work, they are undependable, and so on. I can't count the times I've heard dark-skinned people say, "man if you want it done right take it to a white man."

When many Americans of African descent have money to spend, they bypass neighborhood businesses and head downtown or to the stores in shopping malls miles away. But when their money is running low they turn to the neighborhood businesses for service and credit. When their charitable group needs help they approach these local businesses for support. When questioned about their failure to support neighborhood businesses, they repeat tired racial stereotypes.

They are sad confused souls engaging in racial prejudice against themselves. They have come to believe their own self belittling humor. Maybe they always believed it and used humor to hide their shame.

Here is real confusion. These people destroy their own economic growth by discriminating against their own group. I'm not suggesting that people choose dark-skinned businesspeople and workers because of skin color. I'm saying don't exclude them because of it. As Americans of African descent we devalue our own worth when we belittle `black' businesspeople or workers. We give false testimony against ourselves.

We can't charge others with discriminating against us if we engage in the same practices. Banks resist making loans to dark-skinned businesspeople. Is this racist discrimination or good business practice? It's probably both depending on the situation. Would you lend money to people who lacked the support of their own neighbors? It's hard to ignore stereotypes when many in the targeted group believe them about themselves. Many Americans of

African descent aren't even aware of this conflict in their attitude. Many American consumers of African descent prefer dealing with pale-skinned merchants, professionals and tradesmen. If they prefer not to use the services of darker skinned people, how can they expect other consumers to act differently? Businesspeople will not hire them if no one wants the products of their labors. American businesspeople of African descent cannot succeed if no one wants their services. Americans of African descent must realize that they are workers and consumers. When they bypass businesses owned or operated by Americans of African descent, they are eliminating a need for their own services. They believe racial stereotypes about themselves and it is destroying them economically.

Stop making self deprecating remarks (remarks belittling the group or yourself) at once! Do not tolerate them in casual conversation, jokes, movies, plays or your own thinking. Tell others how you feel about the practice. Don't make a scene, cause unpleasantness or try to embarrass anyone. Let your associates know why you no longer use these destructive terms. Avoid people who continue to use them.

We are involved in many contests during our lives. When playing sports, we expect our teammates to encourage us. During illness we expect loved ones to emphasize our strengths. Soldiers don't weaken each other's morale by repeating enemy propaganda about their weaknesses. Even if they jokingly do so it could give the enemy psychological advantages. Life is your greatest contest. Stop throwing the contest by mentally abusing yourself.

I can't stress enough the damage these statements have on your psyche. You will know how controlling they are when you try to stop using them. They'll pop out even though you've vowed not to use them. Their use is so common it will take weeks of conscious effort before your mental alarm trips when others use them. It will be so hard to stop using them that many people will give up the effort. They'll convince themselves that I'm wrong and that no harm results from using them.

Image

We use words to describe mental pictures. First we think of the words that come closest to describing our thoughts. We can reject them and choose others. We can even choose words giving a description opposite to our mental image. But words giving the right description are the first ones that come into our mind. Your real self-image is negative if these are the type words that normally come to your mind.

People could argue that it's just a bad habit. It doesn't do any harm. They're wrong. Whether made from habit or belief, constant negative references about yourself harms your self-image. You must stop making them. Remember! You have to create thoughts before you can speak. Each time you speak or listen thoughts and images are formed. Your thoughts about yourself and your group are habitually negative if your remarks are. Negative thinking poisons the mind like drugs and alcohol pollutes the body. Don't poison yourself or let close associates poison you. Never be so foolhardy as to pay to have some comic or movie director poison your thinking.

Attitudes

Another section of the book discusses the effects that the history of enslavement had on Americans of African ancestry. I showed how the wrong attitude about this period causes injurious subconscious thoughts, and grave emotional problems. These problems chip away the foundations of a person's self-esteem. Poor attitudes in other areas also cause problems.

Black Culture

A culture has been created for `black' Americans (African-Americans). This culture is alleged to be separate and distinct from the main stream culture of America. `Black' American is an ethnic group referred to by the press and the electronic media. Self appointed and media created `black' leaders also refer to `black'

American culture. American school children, workers, politicians, etc., all refer to `black' culture. What is culture?

Webster's Seventh New Collegiate Dictionary, 1972: defines culture as:

>5.a: a particular stage of advancement in civilization
>b: the characteristic features of such a stage or state.
>c: behavior typical of a group or class.

Using this definition can one say there is a separate culture for `black' Americans?

A particular stage of advancement in civilization

Using this definition would cause one to believe that citizens of African ancestry are at a different stage of civilization than other Americans. This obviously isn't true. There are dark-skinned Americans at every intellectual, economic, and artistic level found in the country.

"behavior typical of a group or class"

Is there a behavior that is typical of persons who have African ancestors? Is there a behavior typical of Americans of African descent? Does this typical behavior apply to people at all education and income levels?   No. There is a common shared experience of oppression. But people react differently to oppression.

People promoting "African-Americanism" also claim the existence of a `black' culture. Many even insist that there is a separate language for `black' Americans. Some people have good motives for promoting these ideas. They are trying to forge a common bond between people oppressed because of skin color. But their efforts help people using the idea of a `black' culture as justification for oppression.

Image			79

Ruling elites take advantage of the idea of a separate black culture. They have used media and social institutions to develop this idea. But their version is a degenerate culture of dependent people. Actions of the least educated, least successful and least disciplined brown skinned Americans are used as the defining standards for `black' American culture. These negative characteristics ( poverty, high unemployment, rampant drug sales, broken families, school dropouts, gang wars, and teenage pregnancy) have become `black' American culture. Government reports, the media and politicians use inner-city-life, black-community and black-culture interchangeably. Now they are commonly accepted as meaning the same thing.

This would be an unnatural way to define it even if there were a `black' culture. No other culture is defined by its poorer, less educated part. The 40 percent who are home owners, business people, teachers and other professionals would be the real culture base of such a community. This is a stereotyping tactic and not an honest effort to describe culture.

Having created this idea of a separate `black' culture and community, leaders make it responsible for itself. National leaders contend and `black' leaders agree that the `black' community must take responsibility for its own problems. This community is defined by skin color, not physical boundaries. Within this logic, brown-skinned merchants in New York and San Francisco are in the same community. Pale-skinned merchants sharing the same building with brown-skinned merchants are in different communities. So people are grouped by skin color, labeled, exploited, and abandoned.

These `black' Americans are degraded in two ways. First, elites convince them that their darker skin color separates them from American culture. Secondly, they're persuaded that poverty and crime are part of their `black' culture. These slick moves allow pale-skinned Americans to excuse themselves from responsibility for the social and economic conditions of oppressed people. Then they can feel charitable for helping "blacks," instead of feeling a sense of obligation toward fellow Americans.

This is an example of how people are manipulated through their group's image. They embrace negativity as they identify with their mythical `black' culture. Like having "Stupid" for a name, people describe your worth when they say your name. Even if you were not stupid you would constantly fight the image of your name. It would cause a loss of status and drag at your self-esteem.

Many Americans of African ancestry do not realize that they have been programmed to see themselves as inferior. They identify with anything African or `black' that anyone throws into the grab bag of `black' culture. For them, people leave `black' American culture and enter "white "(European) culture when they:

1. speak proper English.
2. improve their education.
3. take pleasure in reading or studying non-African cultures.
4. work in a business suit or the female equivalent.
5. attain wealth or earn a high income in areas other than the sports or entertainment field.
6. enjoy music other than the so called `black' norms such as jazz, rhythm and blues, or rap.
7. move to a different neighborhood, especially if it has few dark-skinned families.
8. support law enforcement efforts.

Negative goals seem appropriate to them, because they're confused. First, they believe the idea of two Americas. Then, they accept the idea that all positive things are parts of the `white' culture. The good life and things that make it good are alien to them. For them, all these things must be a part of the white world. All that is negative or bad (poverty, ignorance, crime and lack of self discipline) they claim for the `black' culture.

Only a totally demoralized group of people would reject the positive and claim the negative for their domain. No clear thinking individual would claim the ghetto, poor education, slang and immorality as an inheritance for their children. People with positive self-image claim the best for themselves, even when they don't deserve it. Negative propaganda has destroyed these instinctive feelings of worthiness in many American citizens of African ancestry.

Lacking instinctive norms of self-worth, they abandon logical thinking in a blind rush to defend `black' culture. They have no self-image outside the notion of blackness. Like people trapped in a fun house of mirrors, they stumble from image to image looking for their real selves. They won't find it. All fun house mirror images are distorted. If people don't already know what they look like, they won't find out by looking in fun house mirrors. The same is true for those who look for their image in the media (newspapers, movies, TV, comic shows). These sources distort images. Images of dark-skinned people usually are distorted in negative ways.

Instead of rejecting these false images, many American citizens of African ancestry accept them as true. Then they contrive ways to make these mythical negative characteristics into something positive. They are fictional characters who live only in fantasy.

Fantasies deceive people. Fantasies about cultural purity and ancestor worship let people wallow in warm muddy puddles of inferiority. They hide the need for self assessments and self improvement. Fantasies give people some comfort in their poverty by making their plight a cultural expression. But fantasies are traps. For them to work, people must totally believe them. When they do, they stay in the trap and are resentful of others who are trying to escape. People in fantasy believe they are the independent group separating itself from general society. Truly, society is leaving them behind as misfits.

Self deception is common among many oppressed people. Rulers don't suffer these self defeating fantasies. For them the best of all cultures exists for their pleasure. Either they share in it, or they take it all for themselves. If it improves the quality of their lives they claim it for themselves. Whether it comes from others' labor, music, sports, food, or scientific discovery, they claim it for inclusion into their world. They enjoy the spoils from African and Asian cultures. Their practice of enjoying the contributions of many cultures is a good one. However, some patterns of oppressing people and stealing labor are not good.

Many oppressed people live in poor neighborhoods surrounded by brown skinned neighbors. Mistakenly, they believe that all people with darker skin have traditions of ignorance and poverty. Areas and lifestyles outside the ghetto are alien to them. Neither their experiences, nor their education gives them an accurate picture of the real world. `black' folk are traitors when they move away. They believe that American citizens of African descent should still be confined to the ghetto, even if they have the money and education to live elsewhere. Sadly, they fight as hard to confine all dark-skinned groups to ghetto life as does the powerful minority. These individuals cannot speak for all Americans of African ancestry. Often, their thinking is confused so they don't even speak well for themselves.

Limited by their background and influenced by propaganda, they believe that pale-skinned men naturally live better. So, accepting these men as the natural ruling class is easy for them. They would fiercely deny such beliefs and consciously are not aware of them. But their actions show otherwise.

It's puzzling why bright intelligent dark-skinned individuals, who should know better, engage in this type thinking. They have both the experience and education to know that skin color doesn't make people superior or inferior. This should make them leaders for clear thinking and advancement. Instead, they join the chorus romanticizing black-correctness. They use their education to create stronger arguments for black-correctness.

Young people exposed to it have difficulty avoiding this dead-end thinking. Few escape it completely. They seek higher education, but waste energy championing a defeatist philosophy. Sadly, if they are to escape it completely, they often have to abandon old friends who conspire to load them with racial guilt.

Intellectual growth is difficult when one relies totally on ancestor history for knowledge. It is nearly impossible when this historical information is inaccurate.

Image

Here is a recipe for self perpetuating group failure.
1. Group people by mythical black skin color.
2. Create negative stereotypes that destroy people's self-image.
3. Distort reasoning process and insert inaccurate information. (i.e. discriminate in schooling and hiring, then convince the group that they're dumb and lazy.)
4. Apply the constant pressure of oppression and racial discrimination.
5. Make the group responsible for their own casualties. Casualties are those who give in to the pressure and resort to drug use, crime, family abandonment, etc.
6. As the casualties mount, use their numbers to generate more inaccurate facts about group inferiority. Make it seem that defects in culture and not oppression prevents their advancement.
7. Stand back and watch the group's destruction.

    You can escape manipulation by improving your reasoning abilities. First, you must reject images of yourself made by others. Only losers let others tell them who or what they are. Others, especially oppressors, never show you attractively. Even if they show you with a positive image, it'll be something less than what you really are. People usually rise or degenerate into the image they have of themselves. Although they may never rise to their highest expectations, they definitely cannot raise above them. Whoever defines your image also defines your limit. Often knowing what you are not is a positive step in learning what you are.
    I will explain in detail why escaping from the idea of `black' cultural correctness is so important. Hopefully, highlighting the absurdity of the position will destroy it.

Black Correctness

Here are the requirements of black-correctness.
1. **black-correctness discourages our youth from mastering and using standard English. It encourages them to continue using `black' slang or dialects.**

(rebuttal)
People develop cultural traits as survival tools. Language is society's most important tool. Without it we have problems learning things we need to survive. We form social and economic relationships easier when we talk and read well. More important, we use language to think up new ideas for living better. Clearly, there is a direct relationship between language skills and survival ability in modern society.

Africans created dialects as they learned English. People use modern dialects because they have insufficient command of English. There is no national `black' dialect.

People also use slang expressions to conceal conversations from outsiders. Enslaved Africans and prisoners of war needed to hide thoughts from their captors. Many oppressed groups feel a need to conceal their thoughts from representatives of the powerful minority. Often they see the police, social workers, school teachers and others as representatives of the ruling minority. Gang members use slang to shield secrets from society. Children and teenagers use it to create a world independent from adults.

People are in crisis when they must consistently hide the meaning of their thoughts in slang and dialects. There are times when secrecy is needed. However, only people who feel inferior and powerless need conceal the meanings of their routine conversations from others.

Most people use `black' dialects because it's the only language they know. Intuitively, they know its use limits opportunities for a better life. Fearing they cannot master proper English, they cling to the familiar but ineffective dialect. It is often easier for people to put up with the inadequacies of the familiar and not take on the difficult task of learning something new. Under the guise of promoting `black' culture, they make others continue this destructive practice. Educated people use dialects with the mistaken belief they preserve `black' culture. Others use it to show blackness. `Black' dialects are based on the English language. So the base language comes from a country in Europe. I don't see how anyone could conclude that these dialects promote any African culture.

Children adopt the slang and dialect of their parents. They are handicapped with language that is generalized and vague. More so now that profanity dominates `black' expression. Many children hear these dialects with its vulgarity regularly. They lose, or never learn, a sense of its being unacceptable outside their limited circle.

Their parents send them into the world with faulty communication skills. Many enter school as foreigners, forced to learn English as a second language. Parents brand textbooks using standard English as culturally biased. Bias does exists in school textbooks, but using standard English isn't part of the bias.

English is the language used for national business transactions. It also is a language used in international trade, finance, and education. The world's scientist, foreign business leaders, rich people and powerful people all learn English. It's ridiculous for anyone to believe that `black' dialect provides them with the communication skills they need to succeed in the United States of America.

Learning and using standard English improves your thinking and communication skills. These are skills you need to fight oppression. The better thinker has more options and doesn't need to resort to violence as often. As you gain more command over English words, you gain more control over your life. Even when you lack a teacher, you can learn from books. You can also transmit your ideas to others better. This command decreases the power of your oppressors.

If you have a good command of the English language, why validate a stereotype by using dialects? Study it if you are weak in its use. Read books, attend night school, form study groups to increase your proficiency in its usage..

2. **Black-correctness means one must not show an interest in becoming educated in what is considered the `white' man's world.**

(rebuttal)

The hostility many youth from oppressed groups have toward education is ridiculous and self destructive. I am dismayed by their lack of basic survival instincts. Somehow we must make them aware that education improves their chances for survival. Their free training period for adult living is short and inadequate. When this period is over, like it or not, they must swim with the sharks.

Most American youth fail to understand that only they can ensure their survival. The hardships of oppression should make this clear to these children sooner. Instead, many of them seem ignorant of this need. They skip along with the attitude that society owes them care. They don't realize that society doesn't care if they live or die. If they cannot contribute, society actually prefers that they die and not use resources.

Young people must learn that the world is like an ocean full of sharks. Education is society's way of training citizens to survive in that ocean. When one fails the course, they lose their chance to function as independent self supporting citizens. They may survive, but only from the charity and protection of others. By failing to learn, they hand the control of their lives over to others. We're in a period when governments offer minimum care to people who can't make it on their own. Governments haven't always helped the poor and may not continue to do so.

Gaining maximum skills should be every student's main concern. Anyone who interferes with that education is your mortal enemy. They keep you ignorant by blocking your opportunities to learn. Class clowns and bad guys wasting the teachers' time are your enemies. Destroyers of school property are your enemies. Misguided fools who try to convince you that it's not `black' or Hispanic or feminine to seek the `white' man's education, also are your enemies.

You can liken the hazards in adult life to sharks in the ocean. Educated people are more skillful at avoiding them. But if you're there when they get there, you die there. Poorly educated people probably will be there. Sharks survive because they have learned to swim well. Remember! Sharks are always hungry.

3. **Black-correctness says that one shouldn't work in minimum wage or low paying jobs.**

(rebuttal)

Many of our youth have bought into the fallacy that they are doing slave labor when they work for minimum wage or low paying entry jobs. They are mistakenly confusing two different situations. In the one situation a qualified worker of African descent is offered lower wages than an equally qualified pale-skinned worker. In another situation a person is offered low wages because they have no job skills. The skilled worker is justified in protesting the offer of a low wage. Unskilled workers are not.

Demanding a high wage in this situation is unrealistic. Employers pay according to the skills and not the needs of the worker. Without skills your services are not very valuable. If you demand a high wage you guarantee your continued unemployment.

Change your thinking. You have no value as an unskilled worker. You are being paid to learn. That is exactly what is happening. Until you learn some skills, even if its just heating hamburgers, you are not helping the business make money. As you gain skills, you can ask for increases in your wages.

People are wrong who tell you that `no job' or `street hustle' beats minimum wage jobs. Minimum wage jobs bring in some income, but most important they give work experience. It gives you and your next employer confidence in your ability to function in the work force.

Do not be short sighted and pass up opportunities for work. Parents and advisors must help youngsters understand the value of various options. Working free in exchange for instruction in a skilled trade is an option. Compare the value of the training with the cost of formal schooling and you will appreciate the benefits of the exchange. Parents and advisors must emphasize this to overcome peer pressure.

4. Black-correctness means one must be against support for law enforcement efforts.

(rebuttal)

The reasons given for this stance are that the law enforcement officials carry out the agenda of the power structure in oppressing `black' Americans. Because of this, `black' individuals should not aid the system by giving evidence against other dark-skinned individuals.

Law enforcement officials treat criminals from oppressed groups harshly. Still, this is no reason to protect law breakers. People who commit crimes in their own neighborhoods are bigger threats to it than racist law enforcement officials. Neighborhood familiarity gives them almost unrestricted access to trusting victims. Their criminal activities cause immense pain, suffering and economic loss in their communities. When caught, they play on the `black' togetherness theme. They are traitors to the spirit of togetherness that they use to shield themselves from punishment.

Societies usually consider traitors their vilest members. They usually treat them more harshly than the enemy. `Black' codes protecting community criminal traitors have it backwards. Communities should rally around its victims and cast out its criminals.

Misplaced loyalty is a problem in many oppressed groups. It is another indication of how they often support ideas that hurt their interests. People are more easily manipulated when their self-image is based on skin color. Protecting the "black brother" from `white' authority becomes more important than protecting themselves from the vicious "black brother."

These attitudes cause consequences that ripple through the community. City officials see these neighborhoods as not wanting law and order. Police officers are reluctant to risk their lives or waste resources fighting crime in neighborhoods that protect their criminals. This gives police officers who may be racist more freedom to abuse them. Since most of the violent crime is committed by residents, the neighborhood is defenseless.

Criminals take over and terrorize neighborhoods. Neighborhoods become depressed economically. Frightened by rising crime, retail stores move away. Factories move away or refuse to build there. Insurance rates skyrocket. Neighborhood workers lose jobs. Youngsters can't find work in the neighborhood and are unwelcome outside of it. Some of them drift into crime. The neighborhood continues its downward spiral.

Property values fall. School financing suffers. The quality of the schools deteriorates. Students receive an inadequate education. They can't compete with those from other communities for jobs. By giving misplaced loyalty to criminals, the neighborhood destroys itself. I'm not claiming that misplaced loyalty causes all the problems seen in poor neighborhoods. But it is a major self-induced source of destruction. A neighborhood must be free of crime before it can improve economically.

I am not suggesting that neighborhoods ignore police brutality. There are methods for correcting police brutality without giving up protection. Suggested methods for this are in the law section of the book.

5. **Black correctness promotes the surly rebellious attitude.**

Too many young Americans of African descent have adopted a tough rebellious attitude toward others. They are especially rebellious toward authority figures. Being rude has become a badge of honor. In mixed groups they isolate themselves.

Sometimes they claim a space, then dare others to invade it. These challenges often escalate past surly attitudes when they become verbally and physically abusive.

This attitude dominates the demeanor of many males. Their language, body stance, hand movements and walk all express toughness and aggression. Impressing peers is more important than the opinion of the person targeted. This causes them to carry their actions to extremes, resulting in school suspensions, arrests and death.

Promoting a reputation as an aggressive and belligerent person or group is bad. People either believe it, or they don't. Both cases bring unpleasant results. Many people will realize that your reputation is a camouflage for weakness. Some will feel sorry for you. Others will dismiss you as a clown. People who believe your reputation will also fear you. This will cause them to avoid or attack you. They will not hire you, train you, or want you in their business establishments.

Fear will hamper your education. Teachers will not call on you in class. Questions directed to you will be easy. Youngsters may think they win in this situation but they don't. Real learning cannot take place under these circumstances. It's not intelligent to adopt an attitude that keeps you from getting your needs met. For many reasons, you will be suspended quicker, more often and for longer periods of time. First, your attitude and peer pressure will cause you to defy authority. Second, your reputation convicts you even when innocent. Third, teachers and principals are afraid of you.

Police officers will arrest you faster, abuse you more frequently and shoot you quicker. All the reasons that apply to teachers and principals apply to police officers. In addition, your macho attitude will conflict with their macho attitude. Your reputation for aggression and belligerency gives license for police brutality.

Every day of your life, you give testimony defending the police officer who will abuse you. Your loud music, abusive language and threatening attitudes tell citizens you are out of control. You tell them in classrooms, malls, on buses, and in movie theaters. The attitude and reputation you establish in the minds of citizens will haunt you if you end up in court. It's not so much that the jurors believe the police officers over you. (Although, they probably will.) It's that your actions in the streets have convinced citizens that you are bad and out of control. When they sit on juries, they bring those beliefs with them. It's not smart to adopt an attitude that causes you to be beaten, arrested or killed.

Many use these attitudes to show that they are strong and that they have rejected the slave mentality. It fails for this purpose. People are enslaved in many ways. You are free when you gain control over your life. Fear of the disapproval of friends is mental enslavement. It is as controlling as that of a feared ruler.

Young men are using a slave mentality when they expose themselves to arrest. Enslaved to the idea of resistance, they are unable to take simple steps to remain free. I have seen many cases where defiance for authority was the only reason for the arrest. Usually the person resisted a reasonable request. They resisted an authority figure telling them to do, rather than what to do. For example. A police officer may tell them to move off the curb, turn down their music or show identification. It's not that the men involved resist doing any of the requested acts. Mainly, they resent being told to do the acts. They resent and resist being told to do anything by the authority figure. Often, this issue of defiance becomes so important that they risk their freedom and safety. This is faulty thinking. Once they are arrested, guards tell them to do; what to do; and when to do it. Only a totally confused people continue thinking patterns that enslave them.

Surely young people need to change their thinking. Real strength and freedom come only when people control their social environment. One must be flexible in their thinking if they are going to reduce the unpleasant things in life. Start by eliminating hostility and the need for revenge from your thinking. Avoid groups that engage in them. Control yourself and the situation in pleasant ways.

Education and experience form the basis for our thoughts. Thoughts create what we become. Our mental state influences our chances for survival. Americans' obsession with skin color distorts their thinking processes. It hinders their ability to plan effective life supporting strategies. Lacking rational thinking skills themselves, they can't teach it to their children.

American citizens of African ancestry are too controlled by past negative experiences. They have made these negative experiences the basis for a `black' culture. Children adopt the attitude of their family and friends. Teaching children that blackness means negativeness (not using proper English, not valuing education, being against the police, etc.) is grooming them to be inferior.

Misguided protectors of `black' culture are promoting conditions that continue oppression. People live through different conditions. Kidnaped Africans and their descendants have passed through different periods in America. In each they had to learn new social and technical skills. Intelligence, mental toughness, persistence, flexibility and self-discipline always are required.

Too many Americans of African descent are romanticizing the tools their ancestors used to survive (dialect, slang, food, etc.) This is a mistake. Successful people replace methods and tools as they lose effectiveness. There is nothing sacred about them. Using obsolete tools and methods hinders progress.

Kidnaping, enslavement, and segregation are conditions our ancestors endured and overcame. Poverty conditions are a reality for many Americans of African descent. Oppression is reality for all. But turning poverty conditions into cultural symbols is counterproductive. We shouldn't waste energy carrying them as idols. We must bury them and use our energy for living and fighting oppression.

People should focus on their ancestors' strong traits. Copy their strong survival instincts. Our ancestors used all their resources to survive. They would have seized the educational opportunities offered by the American public school system. All positive opportunities for improving life would have been pursued.

They were flexible people who changed to meet the situation. We wouldn't be here if they hadn't. We honor our ancestors best by following a tradition of looking forward to opportunity.

You need to have a clear definition of what the word culture means to you, before using it.

What meaning does the word culture have for you?

1. Is culture something a person or group practices voluntarily?
2. Can you list the exact cultural traits that make you different from other Americans?
   a. Are there special rituals, ceremonies or ways of thinking that are unique to you and your group?
   b. How do you identify other members of your cultural group?
   c. What is the name of your cultural group and how do you justify it?
3. Can cultural practices be forced on people by others?
4. Are people culturally different just because they have different skin colors?
   a. Does a difference in skin color override other common cultural traits that people have such as religion, economic system, language, education and social system?
5. Does culture change when people suffer from oppression?
   a. Are the methods they adopt to fight police brutality, night raids and poverty real changes in culture?
   b. Does each victory over oppression represent a new change in culture?
6. Does it change the culture of the oppressors?

7. Since there cannot be an oppressor without oppressed people, can the oppressors and oppressed exist in separate cultures or must they share the same culture?
8. Are people culturally different just because they have different income levels?
   a. If they are, then should not all people at various income levels share the same culture, whatever their skin color?
   b. If they are not, then is it right to consider dark-skinned people culturally different because some of them have low income levels?
   c. Would wealthy children be culturally different from their working class parents?
9. Do you automatically assume that people with different physical features must also be culturally different? If so, is this bigotry?

Your answers to the above questions should be logically consistent with your definition of culture. If you cannot give consistent answers, you should reevaluate your idea of what culture means to you.

News Reporting

The news media has aggressively pursued a racist campaign. In the past their methods were open and hostile. "Negroes" or `black' Americans and their events were always presented as inferior to 'whites'. They injected messages of inferiority into all articles. Pale-skinned adults usually were called men/women, ladies/gentlemen or addressed as Mr., Mrs., or Miss. For years all dark-skinned adults were called boy/girl or called by their first names. It demeaned dark-skinned adults to be addressed like a child.

The military has always been conscious of the effect that titles have on a person's image. Commissioned officers are addressed as Mr. or by rank. Enlisted people are addressed by their rating or by their last names. The military also refers to the wives or loved ones of military people differently. Officers are "gentlemen" and their female companions are "ladies." Enlisted people are "men." Their female companions are "wives or sweethearts." The distinction in reference shows the elevated status of one group over the other. Newspapers used these same type label distinctions when referring to different racial groups.

Active protest ended most of the direct negative racial references in the media. Boy and girl as references to adults were eliminated. Segregating news into colored sections of the newspapers was discontinued. This forced the news media to adopt more subtle means of spreading their negative stereotypes.

Ignoring or diminishing the achievements of Americans of African descent are two tactics. When achievements are too great to ignore or diminish, other tactics are used. Unrelated facts are included to lessen the event's importance. Here some examples.

All nations recognized Martin Luther King's accomplishments. His work benefitted all Americans, not just those of African ancestry. Newspapers, magazines and television couldn't ignore his accomplishments. They reported them. However, as often as possible, they included allegations of marital infidelity. These allegations had nothing to do with winning a Nobel Peace Prize. It also had nothing to do with bravery displayed when faced with attack dogs, raging mobs, and police brutality. These allegations were included to demean him. Never mentioned was Hoover's abuse of his office by engaging in illegal wire tapping. Or, that he also used the information at his disposal to coerce powerful pale-skinned men.

Government reports, newspapers, magazines and television routinely classify and evaluate statistics by race. Education, health, crime, drug use, and income levels all are compared by skin color. "Blacks," the reference for Americans of African descent, usually are shown negatively. "Blacks" have higher cancer rates, suffer more heart attacks, have higher infant mortality and so on. These reports make darker skin coloring a defect that leads to these social ills. Actually they should serve as evidence of the damaging effects of oppression.

Reporters rarely look past skin color to the real causes for these problems. This is part of continuing efforts to make skin color a divisive factor in American society. Government and media should concentrate on these other curable causes. Emphasizing unchangeable skin color as a factor serves no positive end. Other more obvious causes exist for these problems.

Poor health is more commonplace among darker skinned Americans because they receive less medical service. Medical services are not as available because they don't have health insurance. They don't have health insurance because of high unemployment and poverty rates.

There is a 30 percent school dropout rate among the 18-19 year old group in high poverty areas. More darker skinned Americans live in these areas because they experience higher (30 percent) poverty rates. High school dropouts and the unemployed use illegal drugs in higher percentages than high school graduates.

Census Bureau figures show that family income was a factor in school attendance and drop out rates.

Family Income	Drop Out Rate
Less than $20,000	6%
More than $40,000	1%

In his report to the Society for Research in Child Development, Greg J. Duncan of the University of Michigan said:

> "Family income is a far more powerful correlate of a child's IQ at age five than maternal education, ethnicity and growing up in a single-parent family." (Oakland Tribune 3/27/93)

Statistics show over their life times, high school graduates make a much higher income than drop outs. The difference between college graduates and high school graduates is even greater. Together these facts show that income and education affect every other area of people's lives. If one can get past the education hurdle, they have better opportunities for higher income. Higher income increases the educational opportunities for their children. It also brings better medical service with in reach and decreases exposure to drug use and crime.

We must be on guard and think differently when given information classified by skin color. Skin color is a factor only because of racist oppression. Government policies prevented Americans of African ancestry from attending good schools. This deprived them of a solid education. These policies lowered the income potential for all Americans of African descent. It doomed 30 percent of them to poverty. We must understand that these negative statistics about citizens of African ancestry do not show defects in their nature. They show us the defects in American society we still need to fix.

    a. Question racial references in all articles.
    Example
    If you read an AIDS report that refers to victims by skin color ask yourself these questions.

1. Is skin color a factor in contracting AIDS? (No)
2. Does skin color make one less resistant to AIDS? (No)
3. Are there any medical reasons for reporting AIDS victims by skin color? (No)
4. When comparing equivalent circumstances (drug use, income, education, sex, sexual orientation, etc.) are there reliable reports showing people of a particular skin color always are being infected at higher rates?

Answers to this series of questions should make the reader suspicious of race based AIDS reports. One should question any social or medical report categorized by skin color or ethnic group. However, there are situations where such reporting is needed. A study could reveal that social injustices are causing increased health risks for certain groups. A denial of education could be such an example. This would decrease their reading skills making disease prevention techniques harder to learn. The possibility of increased exposure to communicable diseases, like AIDS, could result. Reports referring to skin color or ethnic group would be needed here.

We could use the same or like set of questions about another disease classified by race. (Skin Cancer)

1. Is skin color a factor in developing Skin cancer? (Yes)
2. Does skin color make one less resistant to Skin cancer? (Yes)
3. Are there any medical reasons for reporting Skin cancer victims by skin color? (Yes)
4. When comparing equivalent circumstances (drug use, income, education, sex, sexual orientation) are people of a particular skin color being stricken at higher rates? (Yes)

Answer to this series of questions show that skin color references to skin cancer are justified.

Media makes frequent comparisons between Americans of African ancestry and Korean immigrants. These comparisons cause dissension between oppressed groups. If one is going to make such comparisons, they should do so using the full strengths and weaknesses of each group. The common practice is to compare the strengths of the Korean immigrant with a weakness displayed by some individuals with African ancestors.

After the 1992 Los Angeles riots, news reports showed Korean immigrants as hard working, industrious and moral people.

In comparison, they created a different picture of those with African ancestors. This group appeared as welfare drawing, unemployed, gang member drug pushers out to steal at the first opportunity. The idea that the media attempted to establish was that Koreans were hard working, smart individuals, and that Americans of African ancestry were shiftless criminals.

There is a large Korean population in Los Angeles. All Koreans are not store owners and merchants. Television documentaries have shown Korean gangs extorting money from merchants. There are Koreans drawing welfare. Why aren't the Korean outlaws and gang members compared with the dark-skinned Los Angeles gang members?

Thousands of Americans of African ancestry work in the Los Angeles area. There are other professionals such as successful lawyers, accountants, engineers, teachers, news reporters, law enforcement officers and fire fighters. Many of them are landlords and own the stores that the Koreans rent. These are middle income individuals just like the Korean merchants. When making group comparisons, media should compare like socioeconomic groups. Compare middle class individuals of each group with each other. Compare the values of the lower income groups and criminals with their corresponding members in other groups. How fair is it to compare a middle class Korean merchants with teenagers of African ancestry who are gang members, or welfare recipients?

Media ignores a very important fact. Except two groups, Americans are immigrants or descendants of people who fled adversity. They gave up on their cultures and fled their homelands. Native Americans and Americans of African descent are the exceptions.

Americans of African ancestry lived through frightful conditions. But they were not quitters. Even when offered money and transportation as an inducement to leave, they stayed. They weren't quitters. They fought for change and still met the day to day challenges of living that all men face. The welfare rolls, the prisons and drug houses confirm that there have been many causalities along the way. But most have survived and live decent lives. The failure of others of the same skin color is not a reflection on them. Be aware that the media does not provide balanced reporting about events affecting Americans of African ancestry.

Hair

Africans with dark skin and unique hair texture have contrasting exotic beauty in a straight haired, light skinned world. Many of their American descendants fail to appreciate their uniqueness. Having been taught to hate themselves, they try to camouflage these features. Changing kinky hair texture is possible; changing skin color isn't. They torture their hair with hot combs and chemicals. Or they hide hair texture beneath straight hair wigs. Like celebrity impersonators, they resign themselves to beauty through imitation.

Attitude about hair texture tells more about us than all the racial slogans. If we are ashamed of our hair texture, we suffer a poor self-image. It doesn't matter how many titles we assume or slogans we shout. If beauty comes only in straight hair, we don't love or respect our real selves. So, the state of the hair, suggests the state of the mind.

There is nothing wrong with appreciating the physical or cultural features of others. Nor is it wrong to experiment with styles from other cultures or hair textures. Variation makes life interesting. The key is motive. A person who feels attractive, enhances their attractiveness and self-esteem by adopting new styles and beauty techniques. Others, feeling unattractive, mimic others to hide ugliness.

Before the Sixties, women wearing natural hair styles were considered unattractive. In the north it was unheard of for a woman to attend church or any social events with a naturally kinky style. Many men also straightened their hair.

For decades, Americans of African ancestry insulted each other by making derogatory remarks about each others kinky hair. Even in fun they joked about ugly kinky hair. We are in the

Nineties and still we find dark-skinned comics on national television telling jokes about the ugliness of kinky hair. Appearing on television is a major achievement for an entertainer. They could use this opportunity to show creative and imaginative artistic talents. If they wished to include racial jokes, one would hope they would rise above their low self-esteem and speak positively of their physical features. Instead, they play the role of losers. Comics transform moments of triumph into sessions of self belittling.

Internal Group Relationships

There is sexual tension in America because women are oppressed. Some allege that this tension is greater between American citizens of African ancestry. Movies, religious sermons, and talk shows exploit this alleged tension. Each sex is alternately blamed for the problem. If sexual tension is greater between American citizens of African ancestry, it can be traced to the nature of oppression and stereotyping.

Stereotyping has convinced many dark-skinned people that their features are unattractive. This makes them feel less desirable as mates. Society's emphasis on female attractiveness makes women more vulnerable to this foolishness. Naturally, it's difficult for people in this demeaned mental state to form healthy relationships. It is impossible to create loving, nurturing relationships when one or both partners lack self-esteem. Join the self-image problem with the economic problems caused by job discrimination and you have a double problem. Men who cannot support a family make poor partners both for emotional and economic reasons.

Americans of African descent must solve the problems within themselves before they can solve the problems between them. Like a broken record I repeat, you change yourself by changing your thinking.

Even if you still refer to individual descendants of Africans as "blacks," stop making the following statements:

Black men <u>always</u>, <u>never</u>, <u>can't</u>, <u>won't</u> --(whatever you resent).
Black women <u>always</u>, <u>never</u>, <u>can't</u>, <u>won't</u>, --(whatever you resent).

Don't use them, or let others use them in your presence. It's difficult to use these general terms without stereotyping. But if you repeat the charge enough, you'll believe it. Then you'll find group members less attractive as mates. You will always expect the worse from them. People have a way of living up to our negative expectations.

We're headed in the wrong direction in our relationships. We need to put on the brakes and turnaround. We apply the brakes by refusing to use negative gender accusations. Movement in the right direction will come as we work toward positive self-images.

Standards

American citizens of African ancestry increase the difficulty of their struggle for equal rights when they accept certain assumptions. Some of these false assumptions are that:

1. The United States of America belongs to a small group of pale-skinned males. Other American citizens, including pale-skinned women, are only entitled to the rights these men choose to extend to them.
2. Pale skin coloring and straight hair textures are the standards for beauty.
3. Dark skin, kinky hair and other physical traits associated with Africans are unattractive.
4. Dark-skinned individuals are more acceptable when they modify their features.
5. `White' people are smarter.

The events of the Sixties and Seventies show how people's image of themselves affects their drive for self-determination.

Image 103

During this period, darker-skinned Americans realized that pale skin and straight hair were not the only standards for beauty. They came to appreciate the beauty in dark skin tones and kinky hair texture. Hot straightening combs and chemicals were discarded. Proud new natural hair styles appeared. These style changes were more expressions of a belief in their human worth than than they were of physical attractiveness. Of course the physical attractiveness was also evident.

As self-esteem increased so did the determination to claim full citizenship rights. This was a magical time for Americans. Circumstances were perfect for good leaders to turn America away from its policy of racial conflict.

The powerful pale-skinned male minority knew the significance of these changes. They refused to bring America into a new era. They tried to suppress and destroy this rise in self-esteem through intimidation. Those at the front of the movement, Martin Luther King, the Black Panthers, Malcolm X and others came under vicious attacks.

The main target was the growing positive self-image that citizens of African ancestry were developing. Oppressors know that a positive self-image is more important for group advancement than any particular leader. People with a positive self-image will continue to produce strong leaders. In contrast, groups with poor self-images rely on the appearance of a charismatic leader to save them. Their revolts are easily suppressed by eliminating their leaders. Oppressors attacked the foundations for the new self-image. They moved to destroy dark skin and kinky hair as symbols of attractiveness.

Pressure began in the work place. Employers threatened the economic base of the movement. They ordered workers to abandon the natural hair styles or face dismissal. Those in television and the entertainment fields faced extreme pressure to return to the straight hair standards. This was an effective tactic. If workers gave in, they would lose the positive reinforcement of promoting racial attractiveness. If they did not give in, they lost their jobs. In either

case their self-esteem was attacked. People's self-esteem suffers when they can't support themselves.
Employers did not find the natural hair styles unattractive. It was the pride and self-esteem they symbolized that struck fear into their hearts. Dark-skinned Americans intuitively understood the significance of their hair styles in this power struggle. At first, the attacks reinforced their resolve to retain their natural hair styles. Straightened hair became the exception and the symbol of betrayal.

The problem is that we declared victory and relaxed our guard, while our oppressors continued to fight. They continued attacking. Employers declared the natural hair style a safety hazard. The news media and movies worked at making the Afro a symbol of militancy. Military commanders and civilian employers kept the pressure on their workers to abandon the Afro. Media, chemical and hair processing companies continued a constant campaign to promote the straight hair look. The new theme was not so much that natural hair styles were ugly, but that the newer straight styles were more convenient.

Persistence won out. Straightening combs returned. A new oily greasy straight haired style was introduced. A flood of chemical curls, relaxers and waves hit the market. Before long, the stampede to straight hair was on. This time more men adopted the straight hair styles. Natural hair styles for females faded fast. Dark-skinned comics again spouted "ugly kinky hair" jokes.

I repeat. Attitudes about our hair texture shows the level of our self-esteem. We haven't returned fully to the self hatred of the pre-sixties. But we've fallen a long way from the pride shown during that period. Also, the fight for full citizenship and economic equality has become fragmented. Some groups have given up on being Americans and seek separate communities. Others still are fighting for their rightful place in American society.

In the nineties, young people are again making a statment with their hair. They have adopted styles they feel are unique for kinky hair. These hair styles follow a wave of a new awareness about their African heritage. Since many entertainers and professional sports stars have adopted the style, there hasn't been as much opposition from the power structure. Also the new styles send a different signal because they tend toward short hair or baldness. Like sheared Samsons, their short hair makes them less threatening.

Education and History

WE MUST STOP THE USE OF EDUCATION AS A WEAPON AGAINST US AND USE IT FOR OUR ADVANCEMENT.

The education system of the United States is its primary instrument for cultural indoctrination. Since all children must attend school for the first sixteen years of their lives, it's the perfect place to start controlling their thinking. This is not necessarily a bad thing. Every society must teach its youth cultural survival techniques. It's bad when one group uses the system to promote their interest at the expense of others. Misinformation is a potent weapon for oppression when it promotes acceptance for one dominant group.

From a policy of denying education to oppressed groups, the ruling elites moved to a policy of segregated schooling. Now we endure a policy of distorted information. The aim of each policy is control through ignorance.

Racial conflict creates situations that rulers use to gain more power. They generate these conflicts by distorting America's history. Conflict weakens poor and oppressed groups' efforts for advancement. History books ignore the contributions made by groups other than pale-skinned males in building America. If reported at all, it's reported in demeaning and unflattering ways.

Until recently, Americans of African descent were shown only as slaves, servants, mindless laborers or comics. Native Americans were shown only as savages attacking wagon trains.

Conditions have improved but schools still segregate American history according to skin color or ethnic group.
American history still does not show the African enslavement as a kidnaping conspiracy. Nor does it report previous government Native American (Indian) policies as genocide. Africans and their American descendants helped build this nation. Most Americans don't know this because history books leave this information out.

Historical distortions adversely affect the image of darker-skinned Americans. They are demeaned when their ancestors are described only as docile slaves, mindless workers or inept non contributing free citizens. Students believe these distortions. These beliefs allow them to make wrong assumptions that justify a privileged position for pale-skinned people.

Most of us place too much faith in the accuracy of the printed word. We don't use reason to detect inaccuracies and faulty conclusions in books. If the history books show that dark-skinned people were always inferior, we believe them. When we do, these beliefs cause us to devalue ourselves.

American citizens of African descent need to know America's true history. They need facts to protect them from negative propaganda that distorts their thinking. Don't wait for others to teach it to you. Adults don't need spoon feeding. Every house should have an updated history book. They are available in book stores and public libraries. Read regularly. Don't take the attitude that you must remember many names and dates.

As adults you will be reading for information and enjoyment. Passing tests or impressing others isn't important. As you read about inventors, cowboys, military leaders, and doctors who were Americans of African ancestry your attitude about America will change. You'll gain a different attitude about your place here. Most important, this background information will cause you to question inaccurate images you encountered in books, magazines, movies and television programs. It'll eliminate the need for image building props.

Students must not resist schooling because of these distortions. Being aware that distortions exist, they can question the facts as presented. This way they still learn valuable information from their formal history classes.

But we must move quickly to our next step. We must change school text books so that they reflect our country's true history. Facts are available. We must insist on their inclusion into the school texts.

Many people already are working to have the history books revised. They fight to have `black' history included in school curriculums. For years, schools offered `black' studies as an elective. Now they are making it mandatory. The problem with this is that many students resent the addition of another required subject. They view this additional course as an unfair imposition on their time. Backers of "black studies" dismiss these objections. Convinced of the value of these studies, they ignore the effects these negative attitudes can cause.

Teaching "black studies" separately from American history is a mistake. How information is presented is just as important as what is presented. Facts are dismissed as unimportant when presented in the wrong environment. Students study American history. Later, they learn something called 'black' studies. They have two natural reactions to 'Black' studies. First, they'll believe that the studies aren't about real Americans. Secondly, they will see them as being of secondary importance because they are not included in American history classes.

Agreeing to 'black' as a separate program is a tactical ploy by powerful elites to hinder the circulation of this vital information. Placing it in separate courses limits its exposure. It also forces it to be taught out of context with other events of the same period. It delays full distribution and acceptance of the contributions made by Americans of African descent. Students continue learning distorted American history longer.

There is no `black' American history. There is only American history. Interaction between African and European settlers is an important part of American history. Together, with other groups, they built this country. Eliminate the role of any of them and you aren't recording true American history. Civil rights leaders decided that having `black' history taught was better than nothing. This is debatable. As noted above, separating `black' history from American history hinders full acceptance by society. It causes other unrecognized problems. Surprisingly enough, one is resentment. Many pale-skinned students mistakenly believe American citizens of African ancestry want 'black' studies taught separately. They resent what they perceive as American citizens of African ancestry separating themselves from the rest of society.

During July 1990 Oprah Winfrey featured a panel of college students discussing bigotry on college campuses. A pale-skinned college student questioned the practice of having special `black' studies and a `black' history month. She said that these special courses and events caused resentment against "blacks." She asked why blacks insist on having these special courses and months for themselves? This student was born in the seventies and was a teenager during the eighties. She mistakenly believed that the separation existed because American citizens of African ancestry demanded the separation. Nothing in her schooling taught her otherwise.

Students of African ancestry were outraged. They shouted historical facts at her and scolded her. I watched the spectacle with sadness. She didn't have all the facts. But she voiced sentiments shared by millions. Incomplete information causes these false conclusions. This is a perfect example of how distorted history leads fair minded people to wrong conclusions.

Students of African descent were too caught up in their own pain and anger to appreciate the situation's contradiction. Had they allowed themselves to see her point of view, they would have seen that she, too, was victimized by the history books. Then, they could have pointed this out to her in a calm and rational way. They might have gained a new recruit in the fight for truth. Instead, this young pale-skinned female student was made the scapegoat for centuries of oppression. She had to be put down immediately.

Oppressors love seeing their victims waste energy fighting among themselves. The average American citizen of European ancestry doesn't recognize the daily injustices suffered by oppressed groups. Extreme circumstances can make them aware, but their interest will be brief. This doesn't mean they are bad people, just people. Test your own reactions to the suffering of others. How long does a passing homeless person remain on your mind? How often do you act to help them? How often do think of the suffering in other countries? If you're average, you feel compassion. But you quickly forget suffering outside your immediate circle. It's normal for people to ignore situations outside their circle of interest. Maybe it's not right, but it's normal.

If we expect Americans to learn about all groups, we must include them into one American history. When separated into ethnic blocks, people will ignore information about citizens different from them. First, there can only be one American history. Secondly, it forces Americans to learn about all citizens as they learn about themselves. Seeing each group's true historical contributions in context, makes it easier to believe their claim for equal citizenship rights. Teaching true American history, won't automatically eliminate racism and bigotry. It should reduce it.

Although some people will try to cling to old prejudices, it will be harder. Keeping a belief that Africans, native Americans, Chinese workers and their respective descendants are subhuman will be impossible for rational thinkers. Oppressed people will tolerate racism less as they learn true history. Pale-skinned youth will be less likely to adopt the false racial superiority of their ancestors. When thinking critically, citizens move away from discrimination as an effective and justified social mechanism.

In fairness I must address the arguments of those who claim that `black' history is separate from `white' history and should be taught that way. I challenge them to answer the following questions. In which group's history would you place Jackie Robinson, Larry Dobey, or Satchel Page? They played in the Negro Leagues, so this could be `black' history. They also played in the major leagues. How can you separate Jackie Robinson's history from that of his pale-skinned Brooklyn Dodger teammates? When you write of Joe Louis, Muhammad Ali, Sugar Ray Robinson, and others, do you write only of their matches against brown skinned opponents?

How can you write of Martin Luther King, George Washington Carver, Malcolm X, and Adam Clayton Powell without writing about the conditions that created them? How can you discuss the enslavement of Africans and leave out discussions about their European kidnapers? How can you write about the civil war and not write about the efforts of all people who worked for the abolition of slavery?

How does one account for the inventors of African ancestry (Elijah McCoy, Jan E. Matzeliger and Garrett A. Morgan) soley in black history? Their inventions increased the productivity of American farming and industry?

They could answer. We can include `white' people when necessary, but treat them as `white' history treats "blacks." Emphasize `black' people's activities and write as little about "whites" as possible.

My reply would be. Why would we want to copy the mistakes of what you call `white' history books? Studying history is a learning process. Our children suffer when we purposely distort their history. If we provide our children with fact, they can detect history that is incomplete or false. If we teach them distortion, they are doubly confused.

Change

Darker skinned Americans share a common interest. We have an interest in eliminating racial discrimination in America. All Americans share in this interest, but ours is greater because it directly affects us.

We can be defined as a group for purposes of fighting discrimination based on skin color. If we are to function effectively as a group, we must understand the relationship between members in the group. Denying African-Americanism and the idea that we must be a black cultural group is a part of that process. We can see ourselves as a family or as a civilian army.

African-Americanism defines the group as a family. All people darker than a certain pale shade become an extended `black' family. This approach presupposes common ancestors, physical appearance and culture. It assumes members will think in similar ways, have common moral standards and have equal physical and intellectual potential. It results in people being judged by their skin color and not their individuality.

The idea of a `black' family or any other family invites stereotyping. Common `black' and `white' stereotypes prove this. Family also fosters the idea of loyalty to local interest. It also initiates ideas of group responsibility for its fate. This removes the obligation from other groups to act responsibly. Ideas of a `black' family keeps racism in American society.

The idea of Americans of African descent as an army is not exact. However, it more closely describes our relationship with each other. People form themselves into armies to fight a common threat. No other similarities are assumed. Individual moral standards and intellectual capacities can vary widely.

Soldiers who are cowards, weak fighters or drug users weaken the squad's chances for survival. However, since there is no family connection, each person's failures reflect on them alone. Racial stereotyping has no meaning in these circumstances.

Still, everyone is affected by the strengths and weaknesses of others. They should help others grow strong. Strengthening all the soldiers increases everybody's chance for survival. They will teach each other techniques needed for war. They will help the wounded recover. Unlike family, they will abandon slackers quicker. As the civilian force directly engaged in this battle, our survival depends on our winning it. But the survival of the country is also at stake, so its other civilian forces are obligated to support us in battle.

Soldiers form close bonds and have strong loyalties in battle conditions. The bond is strongest when the threat is greatest.

Americans of African descent fight oppression from the cradle to the grave. Under these conditions the line between brother and fellow freedom fighter is blurred. Because of similar physical features, many of us started believing that fellow fighters also had hereditary connections.

People must adopt new living techniques when living under battlefield conditions. When all life is a battle, these conditions and techniques can attain culture status. The techniques of battlefield living become a way of life instead of a means to an end. They are unprepared when the battle ends or the situation changes. This is the situation within the army of Americans of African descent.

We face a troubling situation. We have broken through the common line of segregation. Now our army is divided into squads fighting individual battles. Some are still in poverty fighting for survival first and dignity second. Near battlefield conditions exist for them so they continue sharing freedom fighter culture and loyalties. Others are well educated and have high incomes. Although still fighting oppression, their main fight is for human dignity more than for survival. Most of us fall in the middle group. We have sufficient incomes, so we have time to join the fight for human dignity. Still the closeness of poverty stops us from totally abandoning our battlefield mentality.

Americans of African descent refuse to accept that different situations exist within the group. They even refuse to acknowledge skin color difference and insist on a universal description of black. The poor consider the wealthy as traitors and snobs. The wealthy consider the poor as shiftless and dangerous. Middle income people are confused by the controversy. This weakens the fight against oppression.

The educated and the wealthy Americans of African descent must take their place beside society's other elites. They must be the equals of other elites in character and life style. We will not have eliminated oppression until we are as well represented in this group as we are in the poor.

Many complain that these people are selfish and not living for the cause. I say that's in character with being an elite. We would lose representation in a very important group, if all dark-skinned elites were dedicated to the cause. Their existence makes it impossible for people to think only in stereotypes. Now they must look at Americans of African ancestry when they look at their rulers. America has different socioeconomic levels. Americans of African descent must accept that the same differences will exist within our group.

The poor and less educated are still fighting all forms of oppression. We fail to give them credit for the courage and strength of character they show. We should recognize the courage and skill it takes to live at this income level. The poor often show more of it than rich elites. We need to acknowledge that people on the front lines of poverty have different priorities from those with higher incomes. Their advances are important, because each advance changes the face of poverty.

Separatist

Time and the changed nature of our battle is creating controversy about tactics. Many now are defining our struggle as a choice between integration and separation. For them it's an either or situation. We can continue diffusing our resources in `white' society, or we can withdraw into voluntary separatism.

Separatists say America will always be racist. They believe Americans of African descent must separate themselves into their own neighborhoods. This they believe will bring good role models back within view of the lower income less educated youth. Spend money only in businesses run by Americans of African descent is their other decree. This will concentrate our vast financial resources and lead to our economic independence.

Separatists are wrong. Their thinking goes against the trend toward the integration of world economies. Nations find it impossible to survive in isolation. The economies of the world are interrelated. Nations serve their citizens best when they pursue policies that give its businesses advantages in the international market.

Americans of African descent will learn that the same is true for them in the national market. National events will prevent their survival if they are unable to successfully compete in the national market. I outlined reasons why business people do not have the right to discriminate in a capitalist society. These same reasons work against separatists. The racism driving people toward separatism is also a very important reason it wouldn't work.

Assume that all visible Americans of African descent moved into their own neighborhoods in cities around the nation. Businesses have been set up in these neighborhoods and that is where people shop. Children attend schools there. In larger cities they even have their own hospitals. They have effectively isolated themselves by skin color. They deal with people based on skin color.

People who don't expect the pale-skinned group to adopt the same attitude are naive. Human nature will ensure this. Neighborhoods within cities share water and sewer services. Public transportation, street repair, law enforcement and disaster assistance are other common services. As happened during legal segregation, the pale-skinned majority will make decision favoring their neighborhoods. People do not necessarily act with malice when they protect their own interests. You can be sure that decision makers will always favor their own group.

When we conduct business based on skin color others will do the same. Hiring is a major business practice. Hiring by skin color would cause a massive loss of income from our isolated communities. Even if laws against hiring bias remained, pale-skinned prosecutors would prosecute the cases. Pale-skinned workers on juries would not convict accused employers.

Travel outside our isolated neighborhoods would range from unpleasant to being a nightmare. Merchants could treat us decently or cater to their pale-skinned regulars over the occasional intruding dark-skinned customer. People who lived through segregation can testify to the unpleasantness of that experience.

You could argue that we already are isolated by discriminatory practices.. This is partially true. However, we still claim the right to all the land. Ruling elites are grudgingly yielding ground. When we withdrawn into isolated racial communities, we give up ownership of greater America. This will not stop the racist battle. It only will mean that we have retreated to small blocks of land, our homes.

Lessons of segregation and treatment of Native Americans should show the folly of this notion. They were placed on their reservations. When this land was needed by the majority, they moved them to different reservations. Reservation rules are controlled by state regulations. They need federal and state government permission to run simple gambling games in their neighborhoods. We move to our grave site when we move to isolated neighborhoods.

There is an alternative to separatism. Policies of discrimination already have created neighborhoods mainly populated by Americans of African descent. It is in their interest to support businesses and workers in their neighborhoods. People can support businesses geographically closer to them without being racist. This is exactly what people in these neighborhoods should do.

No matter the skin color of the individual, they should support businesses that provide them with good services and treat them with dignity. They should also insist that these businesses hire from within the neighborhood. They must realize that these businesses are small and often undercapitalized. Even so they should appreciate the services that are available.

Small stores in their area may not carry all the items they need. Even so they should buy those items available before leaving the neighborhood to shop in the larger stores. Also they should let local merchants know the items they would purchase regularly if they were available.

Americans of African descent living elsewhere should support these neighborhoods by opening businesses there. This is not a racist skin color proposal. This is a call to change your thinking. Oppression causes misery, but it also brings opportunity. As victims of oppression, Americans of African descent know the unmet needs of these neighborhoods. Realize that unmet needs translates into businesses and jobs. Life experience gives Americans of African descent advantages in meeting these needs. The goal of infusing new money into the neighborhood and keeping it there is met. As the neighborhoods' economic level improves, the quality of life will improve. Without racist separatism, investors from all groups will compete to do business there. America's principles of capitalism will guarantee this. It will happen faster if crime is reduced and respect for education increased. If the products and services are attractive, others will come there to conduct their business.

An attitude of cooperation is better even for those who wish to emphasize their African heritage. Through research they could build authentic historical African settlements. These could be instructive for their children and for all Americans seeking information about African culture. It could also attract tourist dollars to the community.

Americans of African descent have the same pool of talent whether they choose to isolate themselves or remain in the larger economy. Cooperation clearly has better potential of success than isolation. In the larger economy they have more options and more potential allies. With separatism they cutoff options, allies and generate hostility. Neither method will work if Americans of African descent fail to act in their own best interest.

Discrimination and the Law

Ineffective Laws

Many civil rights laws have major defects. First, citizens are not defined as law abiding and lawbreakers. Instead they're separated into groups by color, sex, age, or national origin. Civil rights laws treat members in these groups as problem citizens in need of special protection. The laws treat bigots not as law breakers, but only as confused persons. Prosecutors treat the accused bigots better than the victims. Even guilty judgments don't bring swift punishment to the bigots. Often, they have the right to enter bargaining sessions for possible voluntary compliance.

Secondly, most civil rights laws are complicated and restrictive in their application. Their complexities make them expensive and time consuming to enforce. Here is one example: An organization may be receiving funds from two or more government agencies. If one agency finds that organization guilty of discrimination it cannot share the information with the other agencies. Findings of the agency can only be used to stop the government funds it controls. Each agency must conduct its own expensive investigation. After all this expense, the offending organization can still escape any punitive action by agreeing to comply with the law in the future.

It is easy to understand why the laws took this form. There was more tolerance for discrimination then. Initially the laws focused on racial discrimination against Americans of African ancestry. Employers, school boards, unions and other officials included as many restrictions into these laws as possible. They made sure there would be little or no punishment even if they were caught violating them. Civil rights supporters compromised just to get some protective laws on the books.

The most flawed civil rights laws are those that single out, or seem to single out, groups for special treatment. Civil rights should apply to all citizens. Today, the term automatically evokes the image of an American citizen of African ancestry. One rarely thinks of a pale-skin male. Many otherwise fair pale-skin individuals view these laws as a threat to their own rights. They work to defeat or reverse them. While working to protect their own rights, they often support the discriminatory practices of bigots. This is a major problem. We need civil rights laws that make it easier to detect and punish people abusing the constitutional rights of others.

Civil rights advocates must consider the very real fears of other people. All Americans must understand that specific compensation for injustice is good. Laws placing groups in a special favorable category are bad.

Many people see "affirmative action plans" as favoring certain groups. Pale-skinned workers believe these laws favor people who suffered no direct discrimination. They believe this unfairly penalizes them for the actions of others. Reverse discrimination is their charge against affirmative action.

They are wrong on both counts. First, American workers of African descent also suffer from the effects of their parents' employment discrimination. Parental unemployment affects the children because it lowers family income. As I showed earlier, income directly affects all aspects of people's lives. Its effect on their education could be the difference in passing or failing a job qualifying test. In addition, the discrimination deprived them of having happy working parental models. Inadequate health care, poorer neighborhood environment and other social and economic losses are evident. Their parents will have less of an estate to pass on. Job discrimination affects a family for generations. Giving job preference to otherwise fully qualified workers is at best only partial compensation for their lost opportunities.

The fact that their parents did not apply at that particular business for a job is unimportant. Denying employment to any person because of skin color, reduced the job pool for all of them. This increased the competition between them for the remaining jobs. The person denied a job at one plant, may have bumped their

Discrimination and the Law 119

parents from another job that Americans of African descent could get.

Secondly, pale-skinned workers benefited for all the reasons listed. When businesses discriminated against Americans of African descent they made more jobs available for less qualified pale-skinned workers. All pale skin workers benefitted from the decreased competition. As children of working parents, they benefited by having better health plans, schools, material items and so on. Their better schooling makes it more likely that they will outscore Americans of African descent on job tests.

Groups have suffered grave economic consequences because of discrimination. When possible, they should be identified and compensated for their losses. We may need different tactics when categories are broad and mixed (male domination of females). Females also have suffered job discrimination. Pale-skinned females gained and suffered from it. They gained when they received economic advantages from their father's and husband's employment. They also suffered the restriction of not being able to earn equal wages.

Government leaders should formally acknowledge past and present discriminatory conditions. This formalizes the conditions and prevents endless denial. Then, sweeping comprehensive changes in laws and policies should be made to prevent its continuation. Past oppressors should be excluded from participation in writing new procedures. These would be school board officials, police administrators, labor officials and others who were proven to have participated in discriminatory practices.

School segregation victims and their children can be identified and compensated. The government has acknowledged that segregated schools provided unequal education. There was clear damage to a distinct group. However, they've never been properly compensated for damages that last a life time.

The disproportionate poverty experienced by Americans of African ancestry shows this continuing damage. Our government must compensate these victims and help repair the resultant damage. Americans of African descent could prove damage by showing the family had endured segregated schooling.

The government should provide special schools for adults who want to correct their educational weakness. Those academically qualified should be admitted tuition free to state universities and junior colleges. This should include free room and board or non interest loans to cover these expenses.

Provide Headstart programs and evening neighborhood tutors for school age children of these adults. One generation should have the full advantage of special preschool, K-12 evening tutoring, and tuition free attendance at the college or university of their choice. Setting time limits for entering and completing the program will help ensure serious study. Students should meet all normal academic requirements before being accepted by any college or university.

This schooling compensation act would be the best way of compensating for past discrimination. It would help the victims and the country by providing a better educated pool of workers. Better education should reduce candidates for crime.

Many people will scoff at this plan. They'll point out that students of African ancestry have high dropout rates and don't take advantage of the present schooling. I would respond by showing that there are reasons for this poor showing. Poor preparation causes many school dropouts. Headstart programs and tutoring assistance for homework will better prepare them to succeed. This assistance will replace that which they would normally have received from parents educated in standard schools. Their parents cannot (could not) provide it because they received deficient education in segregated schools. When adults participate in their part of the program, it will reinforce the children's respect for education.

Some will claim that this is another case of giving a group special privilege. They may claim that there are many poor pale-skinned people who also could benefit from such a plan. Or they will claim that others are being forced to pay for historical discrimination they neither caused nor benefited from.

Discrimination and the Law　　　　　　121

Their claims are wrong. This group was created when the government placed them in deficient schools. They neither desired nor requested to be separated and discriminated against. The question is whether action will be taken to minimize the continuing damage caused by previous government decree. Pale-skinned citizens may call for a similar program based on need. However, they cannot claim it as reparation. Other situations exist where Americans paid for the sins of their government. Government repayment for losses suffered in the recent Savings and Loan scandal is a good example of this. Compensation granted to the American citizens of Japanese descent who were imprisoned during WWII is another example.

Here is a truth I never hear on talk shows, never read in newspapers and never hear in speeches. It is obvious and affects our thinking about our social situation. I can't understand why our leaders ignore it. It should completely change your thinking about government's special obligation to educate some Americans of African descent.

Official government enacted school segregation ended less than twenty-five years ago. Its victims are still alive. They and their descendants will suffer its effects for decades. School funds were distributed unequally, with the greater portions going to pale-skinned students.

Every pale-skinned person in America benefited from the theft of school funds from darker skinned students. They benefited directly by attending better schools. They benefited by having less competition for college seats and jobs. Now they have economic advantage while those who suffered discrimination struggle in poverty. When both the robbers and victims are known, American justice demands reparations.

We demand educational compensation for the victims. This is different from a request asking that people be compensated for the victimization of ancestors. They are continually victimized with each day that passes without compensation. Can you now see how a change in thinking changes this whole question of education entitlement?

When your thinking is distorted you say or accept statements like:

Black youth are disadvantaged (impaired, crippled). The government should give them special Headstart programs to make them more equal.

When your thinking is clear you know that:

The government destroyed the social and economic base of Americans of African descent by stealing their education funds. It must enact programs that will compensate them for their loss and help them to repair the socioeconomic damage they suffer.

Discrimination as a Criminal Offense

Laws dealing with racial, sexual and age discrimination are in a special category. This category is usually controlled by the Attorney General's offices. If the political administration in power isn't a fair one, prosecution for civil rights violations decrease. Funding is withheld, or other areas of prosecution are emphasized.

Placing people in special groups is usually a prelude to an unfair act. Powerful people place themselves into special groups so the can pass special laws which bring them profits at the expense of the general population. Congress does so by isolating itself from social security laws, civil rights laws, and sex discrimination laws. Laws allow lending institutions to charge higher interest rates than the average citizen may legally charge. In California, homeowners selling their home with real estate broker assistance, may legally charge higher mortgage interest rates than those who don't.

Remember my warning. When powerful people isolate the less powerful into special groups it always works to the detriment of the less powerful. Placing people in groups makes manipulating easier. Powerful groups place others in special categories so they can control them. They never do so for the best interest of the group.

Discrimination and the Law

Laws protecting women are perfect examples of group exploitation. Laws protect them so well that it protects them from getting decent job advancement or equal pay. On the job they are protected from the humiliation of public disclosure of sexual harassment and abuse. Male dominated legislatures accomplished this by ignoring the harassment. When it becomes so bad it can no longer be ignored, the woman is still protected. She is saved from the awful situation by being fired.

Two other special groups have been designated for the protection of the family. One is called husbands, the other wives. The powerful husband group has placed the interest of the wife group into a special category. The wife's physical well being falls into this special category.

Members from the husband group give members from the wife group special protection. Until recently a husband could punch, kick, force sexual contact or otherwise attack his wife. This wasn't assault and battery, but only possible abuse of a spouse. Members from the police group try not to interfere with the husband as he goes about giving his wife her special protection.

If a wife persists in making her complaint, the police will question the husband about his brand of protection. After a short chat with the police, he returns and gives his wife some more special protection. However, if the husband gives his special protection to the police or any other citizen, it's called assault and battery and he goes to jail.

A recent congressional study showed that more laws needed to be passed to protect women from sexual crimes directed at them. It said that if they are passed, we can expect to see a change in this situation by the year 2000. That's years away. Women, can you wait that long? Are you willing to wait that long?

Presently, only pale skin males can exercise their full citizenship rights. They are the only group receiving the full protection of the law. They have this luxury because they are the power group making and enforcing the laws.

Change will come they say. We are fools if we wait for it. We do not have to earn the privileges of citizenship. No other group should have the power to restrict the exercise of any of our rights as citizens. No law gives them this power. Their power stems from our inaction. We come as beggars pleading with them to retract the discriminatory laws. We beg them to exercise police power to protect us from husbands, bigots, skinheads, etc. "Wait. Change takes time," is their old song. They intend to wait until we say, enough. Act now!

Present laws and the manner in which they are enforced are unfair to most citizens. If you are a dark skinned male, you face discrimination because of your skin color. If you are a male descendant from any continent but Europe you face ethnic discrimination. If you are a pale skin female, you face sexual abuse, and job and legal discrimination because of your sex. If you are female with African ancestry, or a female of any other color, you face the discrimination of race plus the abuse of sex. Surprise, even if you're a pale skin male, you're oppressed if you're poor. A powerful elite group oppresses most other citizens in the country.

Together we have the political power to demand an immediate end to the physical abuse and discrimination. Within four years we can replace all politicians, bureaucrats and law enforcement officials who refuse to cooperate. This should be our highest priority item.

People who discriminate because of race, sex, or age are breaking the law. However, weak laws allow most of them to go unpunished. They are not forced to give a personal accounting for the great economic, social and emotional damage they cause. We must change our laws so that it is the bigot, not their victims, who ultimately stands to lose from acts of discrimination. Making acts of discrimination a criminal act is the best way to accomplish this. Prosecuting these individuals and sending them to jail is the most effective way to stop acts of discrimination.

Bigots who discriminate and those who protect them should be recognized for what they are, criminals. Then, we must remove them from positions of authority. People must be accountable for discriminatory acts. Organizational responsibilities and company policies should not shield them from individual responsibility. They

Discrimination and the Law

must know that if they engage in discriminatory acts, even if following the directions of another, they will be prosecuted and sent to jail.

Acts of racial discrimination and sexual harassment are hard to prove because of the invisible network of support bigots have. People who don't discriminate themselves, often help bigots conceal their acts. We must pass laws making it a criminal conspiracy to help others conceal acts of discrimination.

Another advantage to making each person individually liable for their own acts of discrimination is that it will remove their network of support. Presently, the law usually prosecutes businesses for discrimination. It may be an individual decision to discriminate and not company policy. However, once charged the company places its full legal resources in the fight to clear its name. This gives the bigot resources that the victims don't have. This is especially true when the state or federal government fails to protect the rights of the worker. In this situation the victim faces the full financial might of the corporation or business. If the person who commits the act is prosecuted as an individual, the law would be more effective. This will force supervisors to eliminate company policies that might cause them to be criminally prosecuted.

Many people will say that criminal prosecution of bigots who discriminate is too harsh. They will argue that reimbursing the victim should be sufficient. There are problems with this approach. First, monetary compensation to the victim doesn't make up for loss of experience, seniority or satisfaction of having held the position. Can money ever compensate for the emotional stress and accompanying health consequences suffered by the victim? The damage extends past the person to their family, loved ones and passes from one generation to the next. A robber takes income earned over a short time. Discrimination robs us of the opportunities to earn income for decades and sometimes forever.

Employers rob us when they pay us less for our work because of our skin color, sex or ethnic group. Our losses from these thefts are as real as those taken in any other form of criminal activity. Why should these particular robbers escape punishment because the business or government agency pays the victim for the loss? Why should the victims of this type robbery have the burden of hiring lawyers and investigators to fight for justice in civil courts? No other robbery victim has this burden.

Often there is no real financial penalty for employers who discriminate. Compensation to victims often is less than the wages unlawfully denied them. Victims only receive part of the money stolen from them. People who discriminate should be punished besides making restitution. Public officials and government workers often suffer no loss at all because victim are compensated from taxes.

All citizens have an equal right at economic opportunity. When bigots refuse us full employment, bank loans, contract opportunities, etc. based on anything but our qualifications, they rob us of these opportunities. Robbery is a criminal offense. The robbers should be prosecuted as criminals.

Those wronged by discrimination often suffer consequences which last a lifetime. This is especially true concerning education. School boards rob children of their right to an education when they set discriminatory policies. When caught, they are usually given an opportunity to correct past discriminatory policies but are not punished for breaking the law.

Changing past policies does not compensate the children. Usually, the resultant deficiency in education will handicap them for the rest of their lives. Some of these children will go back and make up their educational deficiencies. This takes additional time from their lives. While they are repeating grades, their peers are going ahead with their lives. This gives their pale-skinned peers added experience and seniority. We send people to jail for stealing money, why not for stealing years from a person's life?

Leniency toward bigots who break the law encourages others to continue their unlawful practices. Neighboring cities, and states have no incentive to change their discriminatory practices. Experience shows them that their discriminatory practices may never be detected. Even when their are found out, the responsible officials aren't punished. Why should they willingly enforce fair policies under these conditions? It should be unlawful to create or carry out policies that deprive people of their educational entitlement. School board members are obligated to follow the law in carrying out their duties. If they break the law, they should be subjected to criminal prosecution. Then, they will follow the law or go to jail.

Bigots and the groups they belong to are usually more vocal and persistent in establishing their views. Oppressed groups or neutral individuals often allow them to have their way just to maintain peace. Their inaction works to the benefit of those who would discriminate. On public policy making bodies, such as school boards, this inaction is a criminal abandonment of responsibility. The threat of criminal liability will make school board members more resistive to the pressure of bigots. They will resist the bigots, resign or go to jail with them.

School superintendents, principals and teachers come from the general population. We can expect to find the same percentage of biased individuals in this profession as in the general population. These individuals are in a particularly strong position to exercise their prejudices.

An ability to treat all students with respect and fairness should be a prerequisite for teaching in the public school system. Those who cannot meet this prerequisite shouldn't be hired. Except in the most obvious cases, it will be hard to screen teachers for this trait. However, making this a prerequisite makes failure to maintain this standard a dismissal offense. Teachers should be fired if they display bigotry on the job. Supervisors must diligently weed out bigots. Shielding bigots from detection should also be a crime.

I want to emphasis, I do not propose making bigoted thinking a crime. Under our constitution even bigots have the right to their beliefs. If they do not harm others acting on those beliefs, their rights should be respected. I propose only that we prosecute bigots who act on their prejudices and deprive others of their constitutional rights.

128   Discrimination and the Law

Many will say that a person who invests their money in a business should be able to hire anyone they choose. They believe employers should have the right to exclude workers based on race, religion or sex. This type thinking is wrong. The United States of America is an industrial, capitalistic system. Its existence depends on a cooperative exchange of good and services between citizens, businesses, and the states.

Specialization makes our system work. Each person or business produces only a fraction of the various items they need to survive. No business or company meets all their own needs. They need water systems, electric systems, transportation systems, civil protection and health protection. Society provides these services for the common good. Directly or through taxes we all share in the building, distribution and maintenance of these facilities. We use these public facilities with private assets to produce our specialty.

It's understood that each of us, according to our ability to pay, can use these common facilities to meet our needs. Jobs and opportunities for employment are also products of the joint economic effort. They also should equally be available to all based on ability. When people contribute their specialty to the system, they must have equal access to other products and resources in the general pool to meet their needs. This includes an equal opportunity to sell job skills. We distort the system when we allow racial or sexual discrimination to void this guarantee. Discrimination causes our system to becomes less competitive with other nations. It may even stop working completely.

Businesses refusing to honor system rules should be removed from it. We must withhold business licenses from them. The object of these United States is shared economic and defensive interests. If one enters the system, they are obligated to observe all the rules.

It would be beneficial for all concerned if we could eliminate our own biases, fears and hatreds. I don't expect this to happen. It's not necessary for it to happen for my proposal to work. My proposal will work because it attacks discrimination, period. It doesn't call for laws favoring those with dark skin, pale skin,

Discrimination and the Law   129

Mexican, male, female or any ethnic group. It merely makes it a crime to discriminate against any United States citizen because of color, sex, country of origin, age or ethnic group. Laws under my proposal will not create any new rights; they only will protect existing constitutional rights.

Passing laws against discrimination is just the first step. Laws are useless if they aren't enforced. New laws must also direct immediate dismissal of any law enforcement officer or district attorney who fails to enforce these laws.

There are clubs and social organizations that bar membership to individuals because of race, sex, or ethnic group. Many laws have attempted to break up these organizations. This is wrong. People's social association should not be controlled by law. If these social and fraternal organizations choose to discriminate, even if it's based on race, sex, or ethnic group, it's their right. However, we should agree that members of these clubs are voluntarily placing limits on themselves as they restrict others.

Since these clubs are private and choose to discriminate, they should be ineligible for any type of tax exemption status. No activity of the club should make its members eligible for tax exempt status. These clubs should not be eligible for any licenses (sales, liquor, caterer, entertainment). Government agencies must not use these clubs' facilities.

Civil service workers, police officers and other officials holding non political public positions agree to serve all citizens equally. They must be fair minded or they can't carry out their duties. People who are members of organizations that discriminate because of race, sex, age, or ethnic group openly acknowledge bias against these groups. This acknowledged bias makes them ineligible to hold any position which serves the public. Prejudice definitely prevents fair minded decisions. This is especially important in the life or death decisions police officers must make.

Tolerance should be a basic qualification for any civil service job, especially for teachers and police officers. Any expression of racial, sexual or ethnic bigotry should be cause for immediate dismissal. Now, people in these jobs receive sensitivity training if they are suspected of bigotry. This is wrong. They aren't qualified for the job if they don't already respect all citizens. Utterances of racial, sexual or ethnic slurs should be evidence of this lack of respect for that group.

Some will say that the difficulty of proving discrimination makes criminal prosecution impossible. It is true that prosecuting those who break these laws will present a special challenge, but no more so than many other laws. Laws against illegal drugs, the purchase and sale of sexual favors, and various tax laws are examples of this. Income tax evasion is difficult to detect. This does not stop the Internal Revenue Service from enforcing tax laws. People are discouraged from cheating because of the draconian penalties for doing it or helping others to do so. These same incentives would keep people from discriminating if it were a criminal offense.

The same undercover tactics that police use to enforce drug, alcohol and prostitution laws can be applied to institutional discrimination. Problems of employment discrimination would be easy to eliminate. Each employer would be required to have a job description for each position. This wouldn't be unreasonable because companies also need job descriptions for their own use in hiring. Employers would be required to advertise the position and hire the best qualified applicant.

Companies following these requirements would be shielded from any discrimination in hiring charges. If they turned away qualified applicants, they would have the obligation of proving business reasons. This would apply to any qualified applicant and would not be restricted to the historically oppressed groups. So, this would also protect pale-skinned males from discrimination. There would be similar requirements for banks in making bank loans, landlords, etc. Applicant complaints would trigger investigations.

Law Enforcement Control

Earlier I showed the need for support of the law enforcement system. We should not let a tiny criminal minority

Discrimination and the Law   131

ruin the quality of life for the masses. Most law abiding citizens have already come to this conclusion. Two major problems slow efforts to clear out the criminal element. They are lack of commitment from city leaders and police brutality.

Americans of African descent face a dilemma. Seemingly, they must support police officers who abuse their children or close their eyes to neighborhood crime. There is an alternative.

First, they must organize and declare their support for law enforcement. Using rallies, signed petitions and organized marches they must show this support to the police force and city rulers.

Next, they should demand a police review board be set up or changed as follows. Except for administration and support personnel, members of the police review board should not be permanent. Police Officers work for the whole community and not a select set of elites. All members of the community should have a say in judging when they have exceeded their authority. There are no good reasons why politicians should have the exclusive power to appoint members to the review board.

Police brutality cases should be investigated by a panel drawn from a pool of volunteers. [11]

To qualify for the pool a person must:
1. Be registered to vote.
2. Be a resident of the municipality served by the police force.
3. Have no felony convictions.
4. Attend a series of lectures or films that:
    a. show law enforcement from the police officers point of view. Their training, equipment, psychology, etc.
    b. show the extent of police authority from the legal point of view.
    c. show the physical and psychological effects of abuse on its victims.
5. Take part in at least one four-hour citizen seminar discussing law enforcement, police and citizen attitude, etc.

Citizens selected for a particular panel would have to submit to the impartiality requirements of a normal juror. A person could only serve on one panel in a twenty-four-month period. The selection process should be a random drawing.

Cities have policies of not publicizing findings in police brutality cases. Unions and city officials say they are personnel matters and should not be revealed. I strongly disagree. Police officers have authority far exceeding that of any other citizen. They can kill. There is no appeal from their decision to kill. A judge and twelve jurors do not have this authority. The public, grantors of that authority, has the right to reassure itself that it remains in stable hands. If it requires an occasional sacrifice of privacy, so be it.

When city officials resist forming these review boards, (most will) Americans of African ancestry should proceed on their own. Through their neighborhood organizations they should set up unofficial boards of their own. Ask other neighborhood organizations to join your efforts. Do not restrict your pool to neighborhood residents. Wider participation adds pressure to politicians.

Qualify your panel the same way. Use federal and state law enforcement officials for lecturers if local officials will not cooperate. Invite lecturers from the local colleges and universities. Invite instructors from colleges and universities. Show a spirit of cooperation toward the police department whatever their attitudes. It is your department. It is just temporarily staffed by people who should not be there.

Since your board will not be official, police officials will deny your seeing reports. However, the freedom of information act requires that some of the information be released. Have all complaints submitted in writing. Investigate as thoroughly as possible. Don't fail to investigate the complainant and their tendency for belligerence and violence. If you are going to be fair, all parties should be investigated.

Discrimination and the Law 133

Distribute a summary of facts from the investigation. Do not make findings of guilt or innocence. This could subject you to lawsuits. Getting out the facts will help calm the community if most are obviously frivolous. Those with strong indications of brutality will support your continued calls for official review panels.
Present your findings to the city rulers. Insist that they take action. If they do not, appeal to state and federal agencies. If necessary, sue city officials. Be especially forceful about police officers using racial slurs. Insist on their immediate removal.
Cities with and without police review boards are paying millions of dollars in settlement for police brutality suits. Still they keep these officers and insist they are not guilty of brutality. Insist that these cases go to court and not be settled out of court. When city officials pay damages for abuses they deny happening, they are misappropriating funds. These funds should be used to fight crime. Pressure officials until they stop the practice and remove offending officers. Continue to support your police forces. Most of them are good. Good police officers should not be punished for the actions of the bad ones.

Police Support

Police departments provide services unequally and in discriminatory ways. This would be obvious if people's thinking wasn't distorted. Cities are divided into zones. Police and fire protection is provided by zones. If the available firefighters cannot put out all the fires, more are assigned. Even when blazing fires are out, extra fire personnel remain until hot spots are eliminated. Fire fighters meet their responsibility even in poorer areas.
Police services are different. Officers respond to murder, assault, and robbery calls but leave before the situation is safe. Police patrols may increase. But usually not enough to eliminate the danger. Neighborhoods are not flooded with protection even when statistics show they are overwhelmed with crime. Residents

are told they must live with the crime or do something about it themselves.

Neighborhoods having residents who are both of African ancestry and poor are neglected this way. City officials tell them it is their responsibility to stop the crime in their neighborhoods. The people accept this ridiculous claim.

Law abiding citizens are not responsible for their neighbors' crime. If they were, all would go to prison when one is convicted of a crime. Peoples' legal status would be controlled by their neighbors' activities. Americans flatly reject such an idea because it infringes on their individuality.

But these same individuals make the claim that `black' people are responsible for reducing the crime in their neighborhoods. They hold these racist beliefs to avoid official responsibility for the assaults, robberies and murders of law abiding citizens. In fairness, I must admit that crimes against the pale-skinned also are ignored when it serves ruling elites interests. I am just as concerned about those cases.

City rulers have used ideas of a black culture and African-Americanism to continue this hoax. The `black' culture myth gives Americans of African descent feelings of family obligation. These feelings caused them to reject the intrusion of what they consider the 'white' power structure into their communities. Police brutality strengthens these feelings.

Family members tend to feel responsible for each others actions. City rulers play on these feelings when they charge that the `black' community is responsible for reducing crime in its neighborhoods. It works. I have yet to hear any American reject this notion as absurd.

Feelings of family obligation do not fully explain the accepting of unjust responsibilities. People with healthy egos insist that others honor their community obligation to fight crime throughout the city. "African-Americans" have taken all the responsibility for crime prevention, but receive none of the authority needed to succeed.

Discrimination and the Law 135

With true responsibility, these communities also should have the following minimum authority:
1. Control over budgeted police funds proportional to their areas of responsibility.
2. Control over the hiring, training, assignment and discipline of police officers in their area.
3. Authority to deputize and arm citizens.
4. District attorneys assigned specifically to prosecute crime in their area.
5. Control over parole and probation officers assigned to criminals in their area.
6. Control over all recreation and community center facilities and the funds to run them.
7. Control of planning and issuance of business licenses in the neighborhood.

Force the city to provide safety from crime for residents in your neighborhood. Insist that police resources are deployed so that crime rates are the same throughout the city. Do not accept police patrolling neighborhoods with little or no crime, while your children are being killed in drive by shootings.

In 1991 thousands of homes burned down in the hills of Oakland California. Many people died. One cause given for the extent of the tragedy is the narrow winding streets. A judge recently has given these homeowners permission to sue the city of Oakland because of the narrow streets. These were people who had the funds to live elsewhere. In spite of obvious geographic hazards they chose this area for its beauty.

If the city is liable to this group of homeowners, surely it also is liable to the residents of East Oakland. The city has an obligation to keep them safe from excessive crime. It does not fulfil its obligations. Knowing of this hazard to life, it still chooses to spend money in other areas. Is paying money to fix pot holes in the hills justified when people die from lack of police protection? Can the city justify giving pay raises or spending money in any other area until these people are safe?

I say no. You should say no. You should say it in Camden, New Jersey, Los Angeles, California, Chicago, Illinois and elsewhere. Make all citizens in the city, county, state and country responsible. Newspapers, police departments and politicians all acknowledge the crime in what they call the inner city. They have indicted themselves for failure to carry out their duties. Like segregated schooling, this is separate but not equal police protection..

If all of Oakland's citizens have a responsibility for the firestorm victims, they also have one to the bullet storm victims. If all America has a liability to restore the funds to victims of the Saving and Loan theft, it also has liability to the victims of peace and safety theft in the inner cities. If we can find three to six billions in emergency funds to rescue the victims of our 1993 flood, we can find federal funds to save victims from the crime flood. Politicians, civic leaders, citizens and victims change your thinking and insist on it.

Females make up over half the adult population. Add oppressed males to these numbers and you have a group comprising most of the citizens in the United States. All members in this group face discrimination and fail to receive the full protection of the law. We all have the right to vote. We don't have to lobby a small powerful minority for our rights. We already have the rights. We only need to remove all restraints that prevent us from using them.

I repeat. Within six months we can send a message to all politicians that we want change now. Within four years we can replace all politicians and government officials who fail to respond to our demands. In four years we can also pass laws based on the principles outlined in this book.

Conclusion

It should be clear that peoples' attitudes are the most important factor affecting the fight against oppression. No power is strong enough to oppress people who are determined to overcome it. If they have a goal, a plan of reaching that goal and self discipline, they will succeed. The opposite is also true. No leader can lead undisciplined, demoralized people to freedom.

We have a goal of equality for all United States citizens as outlined in the constitution. In attaining these goals we must:

1. Construct our laws and government so that they are blind to skin color, sex and national origin of ancestors.
2. Immediately change all laws and institutions that presently violate these goals.
3. Compensate living victims of officially sanctioned discrimination.

I have outlined a plan. I say outlined, because plans must be adjusted as conditions change. Also, individuals have variations in their specific situation because of the nature of the oppression practiced against them. Self-assessment, self-discipline, maturity and sound reasoning are required of each individual.

Everyone must fully participate in the fight against oppression. You have no choice. You will be affected by the events happening in society. Someone or some group is working to influence society. You protect our democracy and your rights by being a part of that influence. Or, you can drift and be victimized by each new ruling elite.

Each individual has to make choices. Inaction is a choice to allow others to control your life. You have adopted the slave mentality when you fail to act in your own best interest. Most Americans show a slave mentality, because they are willing to allow a small political and economic elite group to control their lives. People don't have to be physically chained to be enslaved. What choice have you made?

Conclusion

Remember. The tendency in human relations is to move against freedom. By this I mean, the tendency is for small groups to slowly take away the freedom of the people. There have been shared power governments in the past. Various African cultures practiced a form of shared power. But American democracy is the first of its kind.

Greek nations are praised for having the first democracies, but they were not true democracies. Ruling elites lived off the work of slaves. Women were dominated. Women, slaves and workers didn't participate in government.

Western society is based on the Greek model. European nations have followed this model in various forms. The European feudal system is merely a modification of it. As previously explained, noblemen and landowners lived on the backs of enslaved serfs. American democracy started out the same way. Male landowners were the only ones with power. It has been a constant struggle to extend power to all citizens. The struggle never stops. When the people relax for even short periods, ruling elites take away their freedoms.

A major choice you must make is whether you will decide to embrace one American democracy, or whether you will decide for multiculturalism and strife. You can spend your life confirming the worth of your grandfather's culture, or you can work to establish a new fair society.

Remember! All groups are here because their ancestors failed to survive in their cultures. They came here and formed a newer, stronger nation. Why would anyone want to transplant those cultures here? If you are so attached to those cultures, why not go back to the source of those cultures? You don't need to establish those cultures here; you can go back to France, Germany, Korea, Nigeria, or other cultures of your choice.

We plant the seeds for our own destruction when we establish each of these cultures as separate communities in America. America's greatest advantage over the world has been its

Conclusion

one government and common interest. We simply recreate Africa, Europe and Asia in the United States by making separate cultures. Wars between nations and cultural groups have been continuous on each of those continents. Need we bring that here? Can anyone seriously doubt that it wouldn't happen here?

Conflict between groups is fertile ground for dictators who would oppress. People always lose freedom during wars and conflicts. During those periods central authority extends its power. People advancing multiculturism increase the potential for oppression.

Emphasis should be on our similarities and not our differences. We should try to find common respectful ways of relating with each other. Intent is the true measure of people's actions. A person respects you if they treat you respectfully within their standards. This is especially true when they don't know or understand your cultural standards. It's the intent and not the specific act that counts.

This is why a good self-image is so important. When you feel good about yourself, you can recognize good intent in others, even when they follow different customs. Also, you are less threatened by difference and change.

Throughout this book I have emphasized the need for changing the way you interpret what you see and hear. You should habitually ask yourself the following questions.

Why?

1. Why are they saying or writing this?
2. Why have they chosen the particular examples they are using?
3. Why has the speaker/writer chosen these particular labels?

What?

1. What are the sources and accuracy of the information?
   a. What facts have they left out?
   b. What facts are they using out of context?
   c. What other sources should they have consulted?
2. What assumptions have they made?
   a. Are their assumptions correct?
   b. Are they making assumptions based on stereotypes?
3. What personal biases does the writer/speaker have that might influence their opinions?

How?

1. How did they arrive at this conclusion?
   a. Are their conclusions supported by the facts?
   b. Have they considered all the facts?

2. How does their conclusion differ from mine? (Your opinions and conclusions are as good as the speaker's unless they present facts that prove otherwise.)
3. How did I arrive at my conclusion?

Point of View?

1. What is the point of view of the speaker?
2. Have they considered other points of view?
3. Are they presenting a single point of view just to prove their argument?

Conclusion

Names and Labels
(African-American, whites, blacks, culture, community)

1. Do I have a clear understanding of the label or word that the speaker is using? Can I easily give a precise definition of the word?
2. If the speaker or writer is using the label/word differently, how does it change the meaning of the sentence?

List 1

African Nations List

Algeria
Angola
Benin
Botswana
Burkina Faso
Burundi
Cameroon
Cent.-African-Republic
Chad
Comoros
Congo
Cote D'ivoire
Djibouti
Ethiopia
Egypt
Gabon
Gambia
Ghana
Guinea
Guinea-Bissau
Kenya
Liberia
Libya

Malawi
Mali
Mauritania
Morocco
Mozambique
Namibia
Niger
Nigeria
Rwanda
Senegal
Sierra Leone
Somalia
South Africa
Sudan
Tanzania
Togo
Tunisia
Uganda
Zaire
Zambia
Zimbabwe

*Estimated to have around 50 major and 1000 lesser languages.

List 2

European Nations List

Albania
Andorra
Austria
Belgium
Bosnia
Bulgaria
Byelarus
Croatia
Czechoslovakia
Denmark
England
Estonia
Finland
France
Georgia
Germany
Greece
Hungary
Ireland
Italy

Latvia
Liechtenstein
Lithuania
Luxembourg
Macedonia
Monaco
Moldova
Netherlands
Norway
Poland
Portugal
Romania
Russia
Slovenia
Spain
Sweden
Switzerland
Turkey
Ukraine
Yugoslavia

*Estimated to have more than 60 major languages.

Constitutional Amendments

Amendment XIV
(Adopted 1868)

Section 1 All persons born or naturalized in the United States, and subject to the jurisdiction thereof, are citizens of the United States and of the State wherein they reside. No State shall make or enforce any law which shall abridge the privileges or immunities of citizens of the United States; nor shall any State deprive any person of life, liberty, or property, without due process of law; nor deny to any person within its jurisdiction the equal protection of the laws.

Section 2 Representatives shall be apportioned among the several States according to their respective numbers, counting the whole number of persons in each State, excluding Indians not taxed. But when the right to vote at any election for the choice of Electors for President and Vice-President of the United States, Representatives in Congress, the executive and judicial officers of a State, or the members of the legislature thereof, is denied to any of the male inhabitants of such State, being twenty-one years of age and citizens of the United States, or in any way abridged, except for participation in rebellion, or other crime, the basis of representation therein shall be reduced in the proportion which the number of such male citizens shall bear to the whole number of male citizens twenty-one years of age in such State.

Section 3 No person shall be a Senator or Representative in Congress, or Elector of President and Vice-President, or hold any office, civil or military, under the United States, or under any State, who having previously taken an oath, as a member of Congress, or as an officer of the United States, or as a member of any State legislature, or as an executive or judicial officer of any State, to support the Constitution of the United States, shall have engaged in insurrection or rebellion against the same or given aid or comfort to the enemies thereof. Congress may, by a vote of two-thirds of each house, remove such disability.

Section 4 The validity of the public debt of the United States, authorized by law, including debts incurred for payment of pensions and bounties for services in suppressing insurrection or rebellion, shall not be questioned. But neither the United States nor any State shall assume or pay any debt or obligation incurred in aid of insurrection or rebellion against the United States, or any claim for the loss of emancipation of any slave; but all such debts, obligations, and claims shall be held illegal and void.

Section 5 The Congress shall have power to enforce, by appropriate legislation, the provisions of this article.

Amendment XV
(Adopted 1870)

Section 1 The right of citizens of the United States to vote shall no be denied or abridged by the United States or by any State on account of race, color, or previous condition of servitude.

Section 2 The Congress shall have power to enforce this article by appropriate legislation.

Amendment XIX
(Adopted 1920)

Section 1 The right of citizens of the United States to vote shall not be denied or abridged by the United States or by any State on account of sex.

Section 2 The Congress shall have power to enforce this article by appropriate legislation.

Amendment XXIV
(Adopted 1964)

Section 1 The right of citizens of the United States to vote in any primary or other election for President or Vice-President, for electors for President or Vice-President, or for Senator or Representative in Congress, shall not be denied or abridged by the United States or any State by reason of failure to pay any poll tax or other tax.

Section 2 The Congress shall have the power to enforce this article by appropriate legislation.

Selected Bibliography

Asante, Molefi Kete. *Kemet, Afrocentricity and Knowledge.* Trenton: Africa World Press, 1990.

Barber, Benjamin, R. *Strong Democracy: participatory politics for a new age.* Berkeley: University of Calif Press, 1984.

Bishop, Morris. *The Middle Ages.* Boston: Houghton Mifflin Co., 1968.

Bennett, Lerone Jr. *Before the Mayflower: A history of Black America.* Chicago: Johnson Publishing Co., 1987.

Burns, Edward M. *Western Civilizations: Their History and Their Culture.* 7th ed. New York: W.W. Norton & Co., 1968.

Franklin, John Hope. *From Slavery to Freedom: A History of Negro Americans.* 4th ed. New York: Alfred A. Knopf, Inc, 1974.

Glasgow, Douglas G. *The Black Underclass: Poverty, Unemployment, and Entrapment of Ghetto Youth.* New York: Vintage Books, 1980.

Kolchin, Peter. *Unfree Labor: American Slaver and Russian Serfdom.* Cambridge, Mass: Harvard UP, 1987.

Marble, Manning. *How Capitalism Underdeveloped Black America.* Boston: South End Press, 1983.

Maddox, Robert J., ed. *American History: Pre-Colonial Through Reconstruction.* Vol. I. 4th ed. Guilford: Dushkin Publishing Group, 1989.

Mbiti, John S. *African Religions and Philosophy.* 2nd ed. Oxford: Heinemann International, 1990.

McCall, Andrew. *The Medieval Underworld.* New York: Dorset Press, 1979.

McKay, John P., Bennett D. Hill, and John Buckler. *A History of Western Society.* Vol. B of *From the Renaissance to 1815.* 2nd ed. Boston: 1983.

Nelson, Harold D., ed. *Nigeria: a country study.* 4th ed. Area handbook series. Headquarters, Dept. of the Army, DA Pam 550-157, 1982.

Selected Bibliography

Norton, Mary B., et al, eds. *A People & A Nation.* Vol. I. Boston: Houghton Mifflin Co. 1990. 2 vols.

Paul, Richard. *Critical Thinking: What Every Person Needs to Survive In a Rapidly Changing World.* 2nd ed. Santa Rosa: Foundation for Critical Thinking, 1992.

Schaefer, Richard T. *Racial and Ethnic Groups.* 3rd ed. Glenview: Scott, Foresman and Co., 1988.

Thompson, James W., Franklin c. Palm, & John J. Van Nostrand. *European Civilization: A Political, Social and Cultural History.* New York: D. Van Nostrand Co., 1939.

Endnotes

1. Lerone Bennett Jr., *Before the Mayflower: A History of Black America* (Chicago: Johnson Pub. Co., 1988); John Hope Franklin, *From Slavery to Freedom: A History of Negro Americans* (New York: Alfred A. Knopf, Inc., 1974); Peter Kolchin, *Unfree Labor: American Slavery and Russian Serfdom* (Cambridge, Md.: Harvard University Press, 1987).

2. Thompson, Palm and Nostrand, *European Civilization: A Political, Social and Cultural History* (New York: D. Van Nostrand Co, 1939) P453

3. John p McKay, Bennett D. Hill, John Buckler, *A History of Western Society, Vol B: From the Renaissance to 1815* (Boston: Houghton Miifflin Co., 1983) p593

4. See p.42 and introduction, Peter Kolchin, *Unfree Labor: American Slavery and Russian Serfdom* (Harvard University Press, 1987)

5. *Before the Mayflower.* p46

6. Richard T. Schaefer, *Racial and Ethnic Groups* (Glenvies: Scott, Foresman and Co., 1988) p.13

7. Lerone Bennett Jr., *(Before the Mayflower: A History Of Black America.* (Chicago: Johnson Pub. Co., 1988) p65-66

8. same as #2

9. *The New American Desk Encyclopedia,* (Concord Reference Books, Inc, 1989)

10. Before the Mayflower p.46

11. Barber, Benjamin, R. *Strong Democracy: participatory politics for a new age.* Berkeley: University of Calif Press, 1984. For suggestions on community involvement in democracy.

> To be truly alive one must grow.
> To grow one must learn.
> To learn one must explore.

African-Americans and Other Myths

Additional books can be ordered direct from Amper Publishing if they are not available from your local bookstore.

Amper Publishing, P.O. Box 882, Vallejo, CA 94590-0088. USA. (707) 554-3515

Company name: _____

Name: _____

Address: _____

City: _____ State/ZIP _____

Sales tax: Please add 7:25% for books shipped to California addresses.
Shipping: Book Rate: $2.00 for the first book and 75 cents for each additional book. (surface mailing may take 3 to 4 weeks.)
UPS: $3.00 for the first book and 75 cents for each additional book.

Nr. Books _____ Check amount. $ _____